Religion in the University

Nicholas Wolterstorff

Religion  *in the* University

Yale
UNIVERSITY PRESS
New Haven *&* London

Published with assistance from the foundation
established in memory of Henry Weldon Barnes
of the Class of 1882, Yale College.

Yale University Press books may be purchased in quantity
for educational, business, or promotional use. For information, please e-mail sales.press@yale.edu (U.S. office) or
sales@yaleup.co.uk (U.K. office).

Designed by Sonia Shannon.
Set in Adobe Garamond type by Integrated
Publishing Solutions, Grand Rapids, Michigan.
Printed in the United States of America.

Library of Congress Control Number: 2018955086
ISBN 978-0-300-24370-3 (hardcover : alk. paper)

A catalogue record for this book is available from the
British Library.

This paper meets the requirements of ANSI/NISO
Z39.48-1992 (Permanence of Paper).

10 9 8 7 6 5 4 3 2 1

❧ CONTENTS ❧

Preface vii
Acknowledgments xi

1
The Traditional Understanding of Religion in
the University 1

2
Rethinking Scholarship and the University 31

3
Rethinking Religion 61

4
Religion in the University 115

Notes 155
Index 169

PREFACE

Contrary to the expectations of some, religion has not disappeared from the modern world, especially not from the United States. In response to the dynamics of modernization, religion has taken distinctly new forms, but it has not disappeared. That presents us with the question, what is the proper role of religion in the various sectors of a modern society: in the economy, the polity, the art world, the university, and so on.

Over the past forty or fifty years, remarkable developments have taken place in the understanding and practice of academic scholarship. During the same period, remarkable developments have also taken place in how the epistemology of religious belief is understood. These developments, taken together, require a substantial rethinking of the traditional understanding of the place of religion in the university. My aim in this volume is to contribute to that rethinking.

In the first chapter, I describe the dominant traditional understanding, in the modern Western world, of the place of religion in the university. In the second chapter, I tell the story of the developments that have recently taken place in the understanding and practice of academic learning. In the third chapter, I tell the story of recent developments in how the epistemology of religious belief is understood. It has been my experience that, while most people involved in higher education know the main outlines of the former story, relatively few know anything of the latter. In the final chapter, I offer, in the light of the developments described in the preceding two chapters, some suggestions as to the proper role of religion in the contemporary university. In this chapter, especially, I draw on my experience as a faculty member, now retired, of Yale University.

What I present in each of these chapters is only a sketch. The dominant traditional understanding in the modern Western world of the role of religion in the university could be described in far greater detail than I do here. So too for the stories that I tell in the second and third chapters, and for my suggestions in the final chapter.

The topics I will be discussing are philosophical. But I have tried to discuss them in such a way that those who are not philosophers will find the discussion accessible.

ACKNOWLEDGMENTS

This volume is a substantial revision and expansion of the Taylor Lectures that I delivered at Yale Divinity School in October 2001. I thank the Divinity School for the honor of being invited to give the lectures. The attentiveness of the audience, their probing questions, and their words of appreciation made the experience a memorable delight. I thank Kelly Clark, Stephen Wykstra, and Jennifer Zamzow for their very helpful comments on drafts of the book.

Religion in the University

❊ I ❊

The Traditional Understanding
of Religion in the University

L ate in his life, the great contemporary American poet John Berryman composed "Eleven Addresses to the Lord." The first of these addresses begins with the lines:

> Master of beauty, craftsman of the snowflake,
> inimitable contriver,
> endower of Earth so gorgeous & different from the
>   boring Moon,
> thank you for such as it is my gift.[1]

The address ends with the line, "Master of insight & beauty."

My question in this essay is whether there is a place in the contemporary university for such a voice as this. I do not mean a place for the poetic voice, in this case, limpid, wry, pared to the bone. I mean a place for a religious voice, in this case, the voice of one who spies behind the beautiful snowflake and gorgeous earth a craftsman, *their* craftsman, master of insight and beauty. Is there a place for such a voice as that?

Everyone agrees that there is a place in the university for the study of religious texts by scholars in the humanities and for the study of religious practices by anthropologists and sociologists. What is not agreed is the answer to the question I will be asking, namely: Is it permissible for the scholar who is religious to allow her religion to shape how she engages in the practice of her discipline?

When we engage in the practice of our academic discipline, we treat our students and fellow scholars in certain ways. I dare say almost everyone would concede that it is permissible for the religion of at least some people to shape that aspect of how they engage in the practice of their discipline—permissible, for example, for their religion to lead them to treat those who disagree with them with respect rather than disdain. So let me narrow the scope of my inquiry: Is it permissible for a person's religion to shape her scholarship? Or, to put the question less precisely but more briefly: Do religious orientations have a place in the modern university?

If it is legitimate for a person's religion to shape her scholarship, then presumably it is also legitimate for her to give voice to the ways in which it shapes her scholarship. So a corollary to the question I posed is whether religious *orientations and voices* have a place in the university.

Scholarship is a highly complex activity, and a person's religion typically draws on many different aspects of the self: beliefs, commitments, emotions, ways of seeing things, and more besides. Thus a person's religion has the potential of shaping her scholarship in many different ways, some of which may be permissible and some not. It will be important to keep this point in mind.

By "permissible" I do not mean *legally* permissible. The way in which the U.S. Supreme Court has interpreted the First Amendment to the U.S. Constitution imposes some—though not many—restrictions on how those who teach in public universities may express their religion in their teaching. In what follows, I do not have that body of law in mind. Nor do I mean by "permissible" *morally* permissible—though obviously there are some ways of expressing one's religion in the university that are morally impermissible.

When I speak of "permissible," I have in mind the ethic of the scholar. Just as there is a certain ethic of the physician, the lawyer, and the therapist, so too there is a certain ethic of the scholar—certain things one is to do if one is a scholar and certain things one is not to do. What I have in mind by "permissible" is what the ethic of the scholar does and does not permit.

Traditional Understanding of Religion

Nowhere is the ethic of the scholar written down. Some colleges and universities put part of it in print, but nowhere is the ethic stated in its entirety. And, like all professional ethics, it is fuzzy around the edges. Thus it is that there are disagreements about what the ethic of the scholar does and does not permit.

As for universities, it is present-day so-called secular universities within pluralist democratic societies that I have in mind.[2] Rather often discussions of the matters I will be treating proceed by talking about the role of religion in *the* university, as if the writer had peered into the Platonic heaven of forms, picked out the form The University Itself, and was now discussing the place of religion in that. My use of the term "the university" in the title of this essay might suggest that that is what I will be doing. It is not. Those social institutions that we call "universities" come in so many different forms across time and space and are components of such very different societies and cultural formations that there is never any point in talking about the place of religion in the university as such. It is universities such as Yale University today, within societies like ours, pluralist liberal democracies, that I have in mind. Very different things would have to be said about the place of religion in the University of Paris in the thirteenth century, or in the University of Teheran today, or in the University of Notre Dame today, or, indeed, in Yale University in the eighteenth and nineteenth centuries.

And as for religion, though I will rather often use the singular term "religion," I am fully cognizant of the fact that there is no such thing as religion as such but only diverse religions.

WEBER'S MELANCHOLIC ANALYSIS

In 1918, two years before his death, the great German sociologist Max Weber delivered a lecture at the University of Munich entitled "Wissenschaft als Beruf." In the English translation of his lecture the title is rendered "Science as a Vocation." That is misleading. Whereas our English word "science" connotes *natural* science to most people, the German word *Wissenschaft* does not, nor is that what Weber had in mind. A better rendering would be "academic learning." When the word "science" occurs in the translated passages from Weber that I will be quoting, it should be understood as meaning *academic learning*. As for the word "vocation," used to translate *Beruf,* one should hear overtones of the religious concept of a vocation.

Those of us who believe that religious orientations and voices do have a place in our present-day Western universities must unflinchingly confront the case of those who insist that they do not; it would be irresponsible not to do so. And never, in my judgment, has that case been made more profoundly—and more poignantly— than by Weber. So I propose stating Weber's case as compellingly as I can in this opening chapter. At a certain point, we will have to flesh out Weber's way of thinking beyond what he explicitly says; but it remains, overall, a Weberian case that I will present.

To a good many readers, parts of Weber's case will have the musty smell of an outdated way of thinking. And it is, indeed, outdated at several points. The understanding of academic learning that was dominant when Weber wrote, and which he embraced, has been rendered outdated by developments of the past forty or fifty years. There are some who quite clearly continue to hold the view, for example, that indefatigable opponent of religion, Sam Harris.[3] But it is no longer dominant. My reason for introducing it in this opening chapter is that I judge we cannot fully understand the new ways of thinking about academic learning that have emerged in recent years without understanding them as reactions to the traditional way of thinking.

"Science today is a 'vocation,'" says Weber, "organized in special disciplines in the service of self-clarification and knowledge of interrelated facts."[4] The point Weber is making with this bland-sounding comment about the goal of *Wissenschaft* is the polemical point that questions of meaning, worth, duty, value, and the like do not fall within the scope of the academic disciplines. The meaning or worth of that which some academic discipline studies does not belong to the subject matter of the discipline, nor does the worth of the discipline itself belong to its subject matter. Chemistry theorizes neither about the ultimate meaning of the chemical dimension of reality nor about the worth of developing chemistry. Individual chemists may have views on such matters, but such matters of meaning and worth do not belong to the subject matter of chemistry. Even less does the conduct of the theorist's life as a whole fall within the scope of the theorist's inquiries. Chemistry does not tell the chemist how to live.

> One cannot demonstrate scientifically what the duty of an academic teacher is. One can only demand of the teacher that he have the intellectual integrity to see that it is one thing to state facts, to determine mathematical or logical relations or the internal structure of cultural values, while it is another thing to answer questions of the *value* of culture and its individual contents and the question of how one should act in the cultural community and in political associations. . . . If [the academic teacher] asks . . . why he should not deal with both types of problems in the lecture-room, the answer is because the prophet and the demagogue do not belong on the academic platform. . . . Whenever the man of science introduces his personal value judgment, a full understanding of the facts *ceases*.[5]

In short, academic learning "is not the gift of grace of seers and prophets dispensing sacred values and revelations, nor does it partake of the contemplation of sages and philosophers about the meaning of the universe." To which Weber adds these portentous words: this "is the inescapable condition of our historical situation. We cannot evade it so long as we remain true to ourselves."[6]

The imagery of fate and of submission to fate runs throughout Weber's lecture; to engage in academic learning in the modern world one must submit to a certain fate. And whenever Weber has that fate in view and the necessity of submission to it, his rhetoric acquires unmistakable tones of melancholy. The melancholic tone has much to do with his conviction that fate has decreed that religion has no place in the modern academy. Probably most of those who accept Weber's analysis do not share that particular source of melancholy.

Weber's academic melancholy was a component within his far more pervasive "melancholy of modernity," as I shall call it. To understand his academic melancholy we have to understand that more pervasive melancholy. And to understand that, we must dip our toes into Weber's theory of modernization. That theory, in its totality, has proved to be a near-fathomless ocean. We will be doing no more than dipping our toes into it!

It was Weber's conviction that the essence of modernization—not its dynamic but its essence—is the emergence of distinct spheres of activity, activity in each sphere being shaped by the pursuit of the value definitive of activity within that sphere. Weber spoke of these spheres as "autonomous"—that is, self-normed. Examples are the *social spheres* of the capitalist economy, the bureaucratic state, and impersonal law, and the *cultural spheres* of academic learning and art. His thought was that when modernization sets in, economic activity comes into its own in what we call "the economy," free to follow its own distinct value of profit rather than the wishes and dictates of princes and prelates. So too artistic activity comes into its own in what we call "the art world," free to follow its own distinct value of aesthetic satisfaction rather than the bidding of ministers and merchants. And academic learning comes into its own in the modern university, free to follow its own distinct value. We talk of academic freedom.

I spoke, just above, of the "emergence" of these spheres. Weber did indeed think of them as *emerging* by a process that he, and countless sociologists following in his footsteps, called "differentiation." His full thought, though, was that the emergence follows a *recognition* of what is already there. Embedded in the very nature of things are distinct values—economic values, bureaucratic values, aesthetic values, *Wissenschaftlich* values, and so forth. Modernization occurs when a society intuitively recognizes the distinctness of these values and begins to act on that recognition. Gradually the pursuit of a certain value is freed from extraneous influences and develops an institutional base of its own.

Given this analysis of modernization, we can now identify a couple of the sources of Weber's melancholy of modernity. One source was his conviction that to act within some differentiated sphere, one must submit to allowing the value definitive of that sphere to shape one's action. If one is a businessman acting within the modern differentiated economy, one must submit to letting "the bottom line" govern one's decisions; those who pursue some value other than profit pay the price of being forced out of business. "Good people come in last."

A second source of Weber's melancholy was his conviction that one's pursuit of the distinct value of one sphere often comes into conflict with one's pursuit of the distinct value of another sphere, and that there is no rational way of adjudicating such conflicts.

Weber's melancholy of modernity had yet another source as well. To identify this additional source, we must dip into Weber's reading of the history of religion in the West before modernization got under way.

An implication of the foregoing sociological analysis is that one's personal religious convictions are simply irrelevant to one's action within the differentiated spheres of a modernized society—or when not irrelevant, an obstruction. If a businessman allows his religious convictions to shape his business practices, rather than being guided solely by the bottom line, he will soon find himself out of business; and should the scholar allow her religious convictions to intrude into her teaching or research, she will soon find herself either out of the university or a pariah within. Of course, there are some general ethical standards that everybody is expected to follow, and everybody is to obey the laws of the land. But apart from that, profit is the sole concern of the successful businessman in a modern differentiated economy, aesthetic satisfaction the sole concern of the successful artist in a modern differentiated art world, and so on.

Weber argued that once upon a time, before the onset of modernization, things were different; in particular, they were different in the Christian West. Once upon a time, everybody could, and some did, shape their lives as a whole in accord with their religious convictions. Once upon a time, there were people whose lives had the wholeness and integrity of being an expression of their religious identity—people who served God with singleness of heart and mind in everything they did.

Weber always presented himself as a religious skeptic, and no doubt he was—intellectually, however, not emotionally. What contributed to his melancholy of modernity was that he found himself, in the course of his vast historical research into the history and sociology of religion, identifying emotionally with those medieval monks and nuns, and those early Protestant laypeople, who struggled to conform their lives as a whole to the call they heard issuing from God. "Inner-worldly asceticism" Weber called their style of life—using the term "asceticism" in its etymological sense of *self-discipline.*[7] Rather than disciplining themselves to escape from this world into the transcendent, they disciplined themselves to obey the transcendent in all their actions within this world.

Though he identified emotionally with the inner-worldly ascetics and their lives of religious and ethical wholeness, Weber was persuaded that modernity has made such lives impossible. Hence, the melancholy. He finds that he cannot share the religious convictions of the inner-worldly ascetics; he finds those convictions intellectually untenable. But the main point he wanted to make was not that point but, rather, that even if one has such convictions, modernization has made it impossible to act on them in the differentiated spheres of the modern world. There may still be people with the mentality and spirituality of the inner-worldly ascetic, but there is nobody acting as an inner-worldly ascetic in the business world, in the art world, in the academic world. That is impossible. "The ultimate and most sublime values have retreated from public life either into the transcendental realm of mystic life or into the brotherliness of direct and personal human relations."[8] Not only has religion been squeezed out of the art world, the business world, the world of scholarship, and so forth. It has no differentiated public sphere of its own. Religion has become privatized.

Many readers will be acquainted with that haunting passage of icy melancholy, near the end of *The Protestant Ethic and the Spirit of Capitalism*, where Weber says that fate has decreed that the "care for external goods" that the Puritan Richard Baxter said should be worn by the saint "like a light cloak," to be "thrown aside at any moment," has become "an iron cage" and will, so far as we can tell, remain such until "the last ton of fossilized coal is burnt." To this, Weber bitingly adds that those who think that the modern capitalist economy represents "a level of civilization never before achieved" are nullities, nobodies—"specialists without spirit and sensualists without heart."

Let me close my presentation of Weber's thought with a less well-known, but equally melancholy, passage that comes from the lecture I cited at the beginning, "Science as a Vocation."

> To the person who cannot bear the fate of the times like a man, one must say, may he return silently without the usual publicity buildup. . . . The arms of the old churches are opened widely and compassionately for him. . . . It's true that one way or another he has to bring his "intellectual sacrifice"—that is inevitable. But if he can really do that, we shall not rebuke him. For an intellectual sacrifice in favor of an unconditional religious devotion is ethically quite a different matter than the evasion of the plain duty of intellectual integrity which sets in if one remains in the academy but there offers feeble relative value judgments. In my eyes, such religious return stands

higher than academic prophecy, which does not clearly realize that in the lecture-rooms of the university no other virtue holds but plain intellectual integrity. Honesty compels me to add that for the many who today tarry for new prophets and saviors, the situation is the same as resounds in the beautiful Edomite watchman's song of the period of exile that has been included among Isaiah's oracles: "He called to me out of Seir, Watchman, what of the night? The watchman said, The morning cometh, and also the night. . . ." The people to whom this was said [namely, the Jews] has enquired and tarried for more than two millennia. . . . From this we draw the lesson that nothing is gained by yearning and tarrying alone, and we shall act differently. We shall set to work and meet the "demands of the day," in human relations as well as in our vocation.[9]

"The demands of the day" are the demands placed on activity within the differentiated spheres of the modern world. Those who bridle at those demands, because they make it impossible for them to give expression to their religious identity in their work, had best leave business, the university, the art world, the bureaucracy, and return to mother church and cozy family. While not manly, there is a certain admirable integrity about that return. Those are the options, submit or leave. There is no savior on the horizon who will recover the option of inner-worldly asceticism. The watchman, looking for the return of the inner-worldly ascetic who acts as such in our modern differentiated society, sees only night.

FLESHING OUT WEBER'S THOUGHT

This is as far as Weber takes us in his case against religion in the modern university. It's a long way. But for our purposes, it has to be fleshed out at a certain point. Weber is clear on what he sees as the value that shapes activity within the modern university. *Wissenschaft* aims at "knowledge of interrelated facts." It aims "to state facts, to determine mathematical or logical relations or the internal structure of cultural values." Whenever "the man of science" allows some additional value to shape his activity, whenever he "introduces his personal value judgment, a full understanding of the facts *ceases.*" What Weber does not do is analyze how, as he sees it, members of the academy pursue the goal of getting at the facts. Let me speculate as to how he was thinking. It's how many at the time were thinking. It was still in the air when I was a graduate student at Harvard in the mid-1950s.

Among the various belief-forming faculties that we human beings possess are the innate capacities to form perceptual beliefs, to form introspective beliefs, and to form what, for want of a better term, I shall call "rational intuitive" beliefs—for example, the belief that 2+3=5 and the belief that the proposition *All humans are mortal and Socrates is a human* entails the proposition *Socrates is mortal.* It was commonly assumed, when Weber was writing, that these innate belief-forming faculties are distinctive in that, when working properly, they generate beliefs in us by giving us direct cognitive access to certain segments of reality: perception gives us direct cognitive access to certain segments of external physical reality; introspection, to certain segments of internal subjective reality; rational intuition, to certain segments of the realm of necessary truth. The content of my perceptual belief that there's a tree over there corresponds to the fact of which I am perceptually aware, namely, that there's a tree over there. And so forth. Because these three faculties, when working properly, put us in direct touch with the facts, their deliverances are to play a decisive role in our adoption and rejection of theories and interpretations.

Obviously these faculties do not always work properly, and we do not always employ them in such a way that they put us in touch with the facts. Though they *enable* us to acquire direct cognitive access to reality, they do not always do so. Sometimes the belief produced—if any—does not correspond to the facts. What leads one to think that it does not—or might not? Disagreement, either disagreement among different scholars or disagreement within one's own system of beliefs.

Given that it is the function of these faculties to generate beliefs by giving us direct cognitive access to certain segments of reality, disagreement is an indicator of something having gone wrong. Contradictory beliefs cannot both be true. Perhaps a faculty was malformed in its functioning at this point: cataracts prevent me from accurately discerning items in my visual field. Perhaps a faculty was not being properly employed: a quick glance is not sufficient for getting an accurate reading of the indicator. The elimination of disagreement is a high priority for those who share Weber's view that the goal of academic learning is to get at the facts and their inter-relationships.

The attempt to eliminate disagreement is also, of course, the attempt to achieve agreement. But on the

Weberian understanding of the goal of the academic enterprise, the underlying value is not social agreement but getting at the facts, disagreement being an indication that that has not been fully achieved. The absence of disagreement with some belief that one holds is not a sure sign that it has been achieved, however. The belief might be mistaken, even though nothing in one's own belief system or that of one's colleagues indicates otherwise.

Probably most people in Weber's day held that the way in which perception, introspection, and rational intuition are to play a decisive role in our adoption and rejection of theories and interpretations is that theories and interpretations are to be *confirmed* by perceptual and introspective experience and rational intuition. A few decades later, Karl Popper contended that science works by *refutation* of theories rather than confirmation. And Charles Peirce had already made the suggestion, late in the nineteenth century, that choice among theories is typically made in terms of which offers the *best explanation* of the deliverances of outer and inner experience. One way or another, the deliverances of perception, introspection, and rational intuition are to play a decisive role in our adoption and rejection of theories and interpretations because these faculties, when working properly and employed properly, generate beliefs by giving us direct cognitive access to reality. They enable us to get at the facts.

In his claim that religion has no place in the modern academy Weber was, of course, assuming that the deliverances of perception, introspection, and rational intuition do not play a role in religion in any of the ways recognized and accepted in the practice of the academic disciplines. His argument implies that if a person's religion were appropriately related to those deliverances, then that person's religion would have a place in the university.

It is sometimes said, by both adherents and opponents of this understanding of academic learning, that academic learning so understood implies the rejection of tradition. It does not. Academic learning would be impossible without the handing on of skills, of habits of attention and discrimination, of styles of presentation and argumentation, of criteria for evaluation. It would likewise be impossible without the handing on of beliefs. Scientists have to trust what their predecessors and coworkers tell them. The practice of academic learning is a communitarian endeavor, fundamental to its communitarian character being the acceptance on testimony, by each participant, of a great deal of what his fellows, past and present, tell him.

Obviously not everything that others tell one is acceptable, however. Those who embraced the view that the deliverances of external and internal experience and rational intuition are to play a decisive role in our adoption and rejection of theories and interpretations took for granted an addendum to the following effect: if, on the evidence of the deliverances of one's own experience and rational intuition, the other person's testimony is a reliable report of the deliverances of *his* experience and rational intuition, then it is acceptable to believe, on his say-so, what he said.[10] The fundamental contrast was not between experience and rational intuition on the one hand, and tradition on the other, but between, on the one hand, experience, rational intuition, and tradition *confirmed for its reliability*, and, on the other hand, tradition *not so confirmed*.

We all accept many beliefs on the say-so of others without any attempt on our part to confirm their reliability: beliefs about foreign lands, beliefs about the past, religious beliefs. The idea was not that we are to rid ourselves of all such beliefs; that's impossible. The idea was rather that, in the academy, no such beliefs are to be employed in deciding whether or not to accept some theory or interpretation.

A Clarification

We do not yet have in hand Weber's full thought concerning the place of religion in the modern university. To get to the point where we can see what's still missing, consider that even if academic learning in the modern university does operate as described, it does not follow that one's religion will not shape one's practice of one's discipline. It does not follow that an esteemed professor cannot be an "inner-worldly ascetic."

In the chapter of his book *Sources of the Self* that Charles Taylor titled "God Loveth Adverbs," Taylor quotes a number of passages from the English Puritans. The chapter title itself comes from a sermon by the Puritan preacher Joseph Hall:

> The homeliest service that we doe in an honest calling, though it be but to plow or digge, if done in obedience, and conscience of God's Com-

mandments, is crowned with an ample reward; whereas the best workes for their kinde (preaching, praying, offering Evangelicall sacrifices) if without respect of God's injunction and glory, are loaded with curses. God loveth adverbs; and cares not how good, but how well.[11]

The Puritan theologian William Perkins made the same point in one of his writings:

Now the works of every calling, when they are performed in an holy manner, are done in faith and obedience, and serve notably for God's glory, be the calling never so base. . . . The meanness of the calling, doth not abase the goodnesse of the worke: for God looketh not at the excellence of the worke, but at the heart of the worker. And the action of a sheepheard in keeping sheep, performed as I have said, in his kind, is as good a worke before God, as is the action of a Judge, in giving sentence or a Magistrate in ruling, or a Minister in preaching.[12]

I submit that a good many of the religious people who engage in academic inquiry in the modern world understand what they are doing in the way that Hall and Perkins express so eloquently: they are rendering obedience to God by participating in the work of the academy. The fact that in participating in the work of the academy they conform to its "demands" no more implies, as they see it, that they are not rendering obedience to God than does the fact that the shepherd conforms to the "demands" of sheep herding imply that he is not rendering obedience to God in his herding of sheep. This is their calling, their *divine* calling; they are doing what God has called them to do.

The person who obeys his divine calling to herd sheep need not talk religion while herding and need not introduce distinct religious values into his herding; often it's enough that he do a responsible job of herding sheep. So, too, the person who obeys his divine calling to engage in academic learning need not talk religion in the academy, and need not introduce distinct religious values into his teaching and scholarship; often it's enough that he work responsibly at his discipline. Robert Boyle, both devout Puritan and renowned chemist, would have insisted that his work as a chemist was religious work. In his work as a chemist he was rendering obedience to God—giving expression to his religious identity. He was an "inner-worldly ascetic."

I imagine Weber becoming agitated now. Yes, yes,

all true; but you are missing my point. Recall Baxter's insistence that one's care for external goods is to be worn like a light cloak to be thrown aside at any moment. What Baxter meant was that one's care for external goods is to be thrown aside whenever obedience to God requires that it be thrown aside. And there is every reason to expect that often there will be such moments. We must not expect that going by the bottom line in business will always snuggle up nicely to the obligation to render single-minded and single-hearted obedience to God. We must expect that God will sometimes call the person in business to ignore the bottom line. In the modern world, obedience to that call means being forced out of business. So too for the academic: we must expect that God will sometimes call her to allow distinctively religious convictions to shape her scholarship and to speak with a distinctively religious voice in the university, thereby violating the "demands" of the academic sphere. What that means, when it happens, is that God is calling her to pay the price of never being tenured or, if already tenured, of becoming marginalized.

Every now and then someone comes along proposing to establish an alternative business that aims not just at profit but also at the flourishing of the employees and the provision of genuinely worthwhile products and services to the public. And every now and then someone comes along proposing to establish an alternative academy in which the participants do not just try to get at the facts but pursue wisdom and debate the meaning of things—as in the schools of late antiquity. All such Romantic experiments have their brief day and cease to be. They go "buzz" and die like gnats. The modern economy and the modern academy proceed on their ineluctable courses. Iron cages.

Weber knew that there are forms of religion whose stance toward culture and society is conformist. In his analysis of the place of religion in the modern university, it was not those forms of religion that he had in view but the prophetic religions of Judaism and Western Christianity. The prophet, looking about, almost always finds something about which to say, "This must not be." "We must not do research on aborted fetuses, no matter how many facts we discover." "We must not think and speak only of facts, but also of meaning." "We must not become so preoccupied with snowflakes that we forget the one who crafted the snowflakes."

There is no room in the modern academy for such scholars as these: *nonconforming* inner-worldly ascetics. That was Weber's point. The only religious people for whom there is room are those who conform. Modernity represents the silencing of the prophetic voice within the academy. Such a voice still sounds on occasion in church; now and then it sounds as a jolting, discomfiting, embarrassing intrusion into some sphere of public life: art, politics, the university, whatever. But outside of church and family, it has no effect. It cannot have an effect. The cloaks we wear in the academy, the economy, the polity, the halls of justice, the art world, are too heavy. That was Weber's contention.

Was he right?

2

Rethinking Scholarship and the University

To read Weber is to sense that one is in the presence of an intellectual giant. Nonetheless, I judge that in his melancholic view about the place of religion in the modern university he got it wrong. It's true that religious orientations and voices are sometimes squeezed out of the university or marginalized within. But when that happens, it's not because of the relentless workings of the autonomous sphere of academic learning in the modern world but for such contingent, all-too-human reasons as misunderstanding, resentment, bias, hostility, and the like—these sometimes evoked by a religious voice that is itself resentful and hostile. That the academy richly manifests our human fallenness is beyond doubt. That it just grinds away in accord with its own neutral internal dynamics for getting at the facts, I do not believe.

In this chapter, I propose to tell a story about the extraordinary changes that have taken place over the past fifty or so years in the understanding and practice of academic learning—changes that, when taken together, make Weber's understanding, typical for his time, seem musty and implausible. It has been my privilege, and that of my generation, to have lived through an intellectual revolution.

The story I will tell of the changes that have taken place is brief—sufficient for our purposes, but no more than that. And it's selective in the way that every story about some cultural development is selective, but also selective in that I will include only those changes in understanding and practice that I judge to be well-grounded. Some writers have argued that truth should no longer be regarded as the goal of the academic enterprise; we should settle for what is useful or interesting. I firmly disagree, so this change in understanding will not be included in the story I tell.[1] The changes I highlight are those I think we must take seriously in our rethinking of the place of religion in the university.

There are some who continue to think along Weberian lines. They concede that, over the past fifty or so years, there have indeed been the remarkable changes in understanding and practice that I describe. But they insist that, one and all, these have been misguided and should be undone. Along the way, I will say some things in defense of my claim that we should accept the changes in understanding and practice that I highlight. But in each case, a great deal more could be said in defense than I will say here.

THEORY UNDERDETERMINED BY EXPERIENTIAL EVIDENCE

Around fifty years ago, a group of scholars who were trained as natural scientists, philosophers, and historians —all of those—took the step of studying in detail episodes from the history of modern Western natural science so as to discern the "logic" embedded in those episodes. A student today sees nothing unusual in that. But before this development got under way, most philosophers of the time who talked about the logic of science did so without looking in detail at actual episodes from the history of natural science so as to discern their logic. As I observed in the preceding chapter, some held that the role of experience is to *confirm* theories, Karl Popper and his followers held that its role is to *refute* theories, and a few favored the suggestion of Charles Peirce that scientists choose those theories that they judge to be the *best explanations* of experience. The knowledge of the history of science that those who held these views possessed was usually casually acquired and skimpy in content. There was a reason for that: philosophers were talking about the ideal type, Science Itself. They were not talking about the messy social practice of science as it occurs in history.

Thomas Kuhn became the most famous of those who left the bright realm of Platonic forms to enter the cave. Distinguishing between what he called "normal" and "revolutionary" science, Kuhn focused his attention on the latter in his well-known book, *The Structure of Scientific Revolutions.*[2] He concluded that evidence does not play a determinative role in scientific revolutions: it does not refute the old theory, nor does it confirm the new theory. What happens, instead, is that there is a shift of "paradigm," as Kuhn famously called it. A scientific revolution occurs when the evidence is viewed through the lens of a new theory. After Kuhn, the same basic point has been made over and over from a wide variety of different angles. It is often put thus: in the actual practice of natural science, evidence underdetermines theory.[3]

A confirmed Platonist does not regard contingencies of what transpires in the cave as refuting his views about the Forms. But as the discussion prompted by Kuhn's book proceeded, it became more and more evident that we are dealing here not with contingencies but with necessities. In the nature of the case, perceptual evidence *cannot* be the sole determinant of theory—for a variety of reasons. It remains relevant, of course; at a minimum, a theory must not contradict the deliverances of perception. But that requirement can usually be met by a number of distinct theories. The role that perceptual evidence plays in theory-choice neither is, nor could be, anything so simple, elegant, and uniform as confirmation or refutation.

I have put the point negatively: evidence underdetermines theory. But scientists do, of course, choose one theory over another. Since evidence alone does not determine theory, some properties of theories valued by scientists, in addition to that of compatibility with perceptual evidence, must be shaping their choices: simplicity, elegance, explanatory power, conservatism, and the like. A key component in the Weberian understanding has crumbled. The deliverances of perception, introspection, and rational intuition underdetermine theory. Fidelity to experience and reason often leaves us with options as to which theory to accept.

I spoke above of "properties of theories valued by scientists." Some writers on these matters suggest that scientists choose the theories that make them feel good. The biologist John Tyler Bonner, a pioneer in the use of slime molds to understand evolution, writes, "As has so often been pointed out in the past, a good explanation is one that gives some inner satisfaction."[4] Sir Denys Haigh Wilkinson, known for his work in nuclear physics, remarks, "Even on scientific questions, ultimately we cannot do more than say 'this makes me feel good; this is how it has to be.'"[5] And Wolfgang Pauli, pioneer in quantum physics and winner of the Nobel Prize in physics, says, "the deepest pleasure in science comes from finding . . . a home for some deeply felt, deeply held image."[6]

I feel confident in saying that no scientist accepts a theory just because it makes him feel good, nor would any scientist explain to another that his reason for accepting a certain theory was that it made him feel good. Always there is something *about the theory* that the scientist prizes—some property that a competing theory lacks, or that it has to a lesser degree.

Here is the place to disavow a conclusion that some have drawn from the recognition that evidence underdetermines theory. Some have concluded that there is no ready-made reality, no way things are apart from how we construe them, only ways of construing things. Interpretation goes all the way down. Philosophers commonly call this position "metaphysical anti-realism"; social scientists more often call it "the social construction of reality," from a well-known 1966 book of that title by Peter Berger and Thomas Luckmann.

In an essay of mine that I titled "The World Ready-Made," I argue that not only is metaphysical anti-realism not implied by the fact that evidence underdetermines theory. The position itself is incoherent; it cannot possibly be true. (It would take us on too long a detour were I to rehearse my argument here.)[7] There is a ready-made reality. The fact that we never just "drink it in" but always interpret it does not imply the contrary, nor do the additional facts that there are different ways of interpreting the same segment of reality and that these are often shaped by what we value.[8]

JUDGMENTS OF SIGNIFICANCE IN THE WRITING OF HISTORY

The first edition of Kuhn's book appeared in 1962. Two years earlier, in 1960, an event of equal significance for our purposes was the publication of the first edition of Hans-Georg Gadamer's *Wahrheit und Methode—Truth and Method*.[9] Whereas Kuhn's discussion was about modern natural science, Gadamer's was about interpretation —mainly text interpretation, but also legal and historical interpretation. His book was far more complex and multifaceted than Kuhn's; several distinct themes, not all fitting well together, were in play, sometimes resulting in extreme density of thought and style.

There is a main theme that comes through clearly, however. That theme is Gadamer's opposition to the understanding of interpretation that he attributed to the nineteenth-century German theologian Friedrich Schleiermacher, namely, that a person prepares for engaging in interpretation by putting a padlock on the storehouse of beliefs and interests he has acquired by way of his induction into uncritically accepted tradition and then, that done, proceeds to employ what Gadamer calls his "homogeneous human nature" to interpret the text. It's a near-cousin of the view I presented in the preceding chapter when I fleshed out what Weber says with what he and most people at the time assumed to be the "logic" of the *Wissenschaften* and the corresponding self-discipline of the practitioner.

Gadamer's attack on this view was multipronged; let me take note of two of the prongs. Begin with his remarks on the way in which interpretation enters into the writing of history and on the nature of that interpretation. The writing of the history of some event or process presupposes the availability of a chronicle of what happened. But a chronicle is not yet a history; what has to be added is significance. Of course, it never goes in the additive fashion that this way of putting it suggests. Initial judgments of significance shape the historian's assembly of a chronicle, the resulting chronicle leads him to alter his initial judgments of significance, those refined judgments of significance lead him to assemble a more refined chronicle—and so it goes until, if all goes well, an equilibrium of chronicle and significance is achieved.

Gadamer's discussion blended together two distinct sorts of significance; let me unravel them. One is the sort of significance that consists of the causal consequences of events. The Treaty of Versailles is significant for having produced deep resentment in Germany, which eventually led to World War II, which in turn led to— and so forth, on and on. The causal significance of the Treaty of Versailles is never finished—never all there.

For our purposes, the other sort of significance is more important. The historian is always and unavoidably operating with judgments of what is important *for him* and *for us*. Suppose, for example, that a historian sets about writing a history of Yale University in the twentieth century. He will have to decide which facts from Yale's past to narrate, and judgments of importance will perforce play a role in that decision. Other factors will also play a role, for example, how well some purported event is attested. But judgments of importance are unavoidable; and different judgments of importance will yield different narratives. Was the admission of Jews to Yale important? If so, that will be a component of his narrative; otherwise, not. Was the admission of women important? If so, that will be a component. Is it important that Yale continues to have a divinity school? If so, that will be a component.

What lies before us now is a remarkable convergence between this point of Gadamer's and the point we drew from the work of Kuhn and his cohorts. *Wissenschaft* is unavoidably shaped by values that go well beyond that of being faithful to the experienced facts. Many different theories and narratives fit the evidence. We choose the ones that comport with what we value.

PRIVILEGED COGNITIVE ACCESS TO TEXTS

A second prong of Gadamer's attack on the understanding of interpretation that he attributed to Schleiermacher goes beyond anything explicit in the work of Kuhn and his cohorts. What enables us to interpret texts, Gadamer argued, is that we bring with us to the event of interpretation beliefs and expectations—Gadamer called them "prejudgments"—concerning the meaning of the words in the text and, more important, concerning the text's propositional content. My own view is that we also bring with us beliefs concerning the author, specifically, beliefs as to what the author would have been likely to say with those words in the situation in which he authorized them. Gadamer is a proponent of textual-sense interpretation; I am a proponent of what I call "authorial discourse" interpretation.[10] But we can set that disagreement off to the side on this occasion, fundamental though it is for understanding how interpretation works. Both of us hold that interpretation can be performed only by employing beliefs brought to the act of interpretation—beliefs that include but go beyond the meaning of the words in the text.

How does one acquire the relevant beliefs? It's in his answer to this question that Gadamer goes beyond anything explicit in Kuhn and company. One acquires them by being inducted into a cultural tradition that links one to the text. I would again add a qualification: we also get some from personal experience. But Gadamer is surely right in his claim that induction into a cultural tradition that links one to the text is indispensable to how we normally interpret texts. It's because there is a chain of tradition between the texts of Augustine and myself that I can interpret those texts in the way I do. As Gadamer puts it in one of the apothegms that pop up every now and then in his book and that contributed greatly to its popularity: interpretation is "an event within tradition."

It proves possible to interpret texts when there is no chain of tradition linking the interpreter to the text;

witness recent successes in the interpretation of Inca texts. Observing how such interpretation proceeds makes clear, however, that all of the interpretation that most of us do, and most of the interpretation that all of us do, takes place within a cultural tradition that links one to the text. And who would be so foolish as to rise up and say that though that is how it does go, it's not how it should go?

The deep import, as I see it, of this part of Gadamer's discussion, is that induction into a cultural tradition, when combined with perceptual and introspective experience and rational intuition, sometimes give one privileged cognitive access to aspects of reality that would otherwise be all but inaccessible—access to what Augustine was saying in *The Confessions*, for example. Thus another component in the Weberian understanding crumbles. The Weberian understanding holds that it is not tradition but inner and outer experience, plus rational intuition, that give us direct cognitive access to reality. Too simple! It's true, of course, that tradition sometimes inhibits access to reality. Gadamer's point is that often it enables access.

The Acceptance of Particularity
in the Academy

Not long after the pair, *The Structure of Scientific Revolutions* and *Truth and Method*, appeared and began making waves, something else began happening that may well, over the long haul, prove of even greater significance. Historically, the university in the modern West has been populated in overwhelming proportions by white Eurocentric middle-class males—in the case of the United States and its premier institutions, add "Protestant." Slowly, as the result of various liberation movements in society generally, that proportion changed, so that significant numbers of the once-excluded began to hold university positions.

Fifty or so years ago, members of previously excluded groups who had found their way into the academy reached a critical mass and were emboldened to say what they had long felt if not thought, or thought if not said, namely, that it is sheer ideology to suppose that those who enjoyed hegemony in the academy were simply employing their "homogeneous human nature" as perceiving, introspecting, and rationally intuiting human beings to get at the facts. The learning of the modern

Western academy reflected the social, ethnic, racial, religious, and gender identities of those who peopled it, namely, white Eurocentric middle-class males. The reason for their dominance in the academy was not that, for some inscrutable reason, they and they alone proved capable of getting at the facts. The reason was that they were in positions of power in the academy.

The academy is an arena in which experiments are performed, discussions conducted, poems interpreted, arguments offered. But it is also an arena in which power is exercised by those who are in a position to do so—intellectual power, of course, but also social power. It's exercised—almost invisibly—in the form of determining and applying criteria of admission to the academy, and in the form of setting standards of competence: which sorts of arguments are better, which types of research merit support, which modes of presentation are to be preferred. It's exercised, more visibly, in the form of winks, nods, the knowing look. Weber's concern in his Munich lecture was the use of the lectern as a bully pulpit. There are other, more subtle, ways of exercising social power in the academy than using the lectern as a bully pulpit.

This point, so far, is only an analysis of how the academy in the United States and Europe has in fact operated. In that respect, it's like the contributions of Kuhn and Gadamer: nothing changed in their wake, other than that we have come to understand differently what we were doing all along. Gadamer repeatedly insisted that he was not urging anybody to do anything different but was instead presenting a different analysis of how interpretation is and must be practiced. But in the case before us, a funny thing happened. The academy changed its practices.

The most visible change is that there is now a wealth of research and instruction explicitly shaped by the interests, values, convictions, and sensibilities characteristic of particular social, ethnic, racial, and gender identities: feminist epistemology, black sociology, liberation theology, gay literary criticism, Muslim hermeneutics. In many colleges and universities, such research and instruction now enjoy an institutional base in the form of programs and centers of various sorts: programs for feminist studies, centers for African American studies, and the like. When I was a graduate student at Harvard in the 1950s, no one spoke of such things as feminist epistemology and black sociology. Had anyone proposed such a thing, her proposal would have been greeted with a blend of incomprehension, horror, and derision. Feminist epistemology, whatever it might be, would be biased epistemology, and hence unacceptable in the academy! The change has been rapid and enormous.

It was by no means to be expected that the claim that the academy had not been operating in generically human fashion would have, as one of its most striking results, the emergence of research and instruction explicitly shaped by the interests, values, convictions, and sensibilities characteristic of particular identities of the sort I have mentioned—let me call them *character-identities*. The reasonable expectation would have been that the academy would either fend off the charge—"it's crazy to say that there is something male about symbolic logic"— or feel chastised and resolve to do better. Some people have in fact responded in one or the other of those two ways. But, as I noted above, many colleges and universities have instead responded by adding explicitly particularist studies to their programs—while saving themselves the trouble that would ensue were they to take the further step of institutionally declaring that *all* learning is particularist in character, proceeding then to pair off feminist epistemology with avowedly male epistemology, black history with explicitly white history, liberation theology with explicitly imperialist theology, and so forth.

Those who oppose this development see it as caving in to the pressures of political correctness; those who favor it see it as the democratizing of the academy. Whatever the merits of those views, I affirm the legitimacy and importance of this acceptance of particularity in academic learning, with its consequent pluralizing of the academy.

One of the consequences of living in a liberal democratic polity is that there is, among us, enormous diversity in the values we embrace and the convictions we live by. Consider, once again, the historian who writes a history of Yale in the twentieth century. Suppose he decides to give prominence to the opening up of Yale to others than white Protestant males. Suppose, further, that he regards this development not only as important but good, and narrates it as such. Almost certainly there are others in our society who regard this same stretch of history in a very different light. Some of those, if they were writing a history of Yale in the twentieth century, would highlight Yale's loss of its religious roots.

In short, if consensus on what is significant is required, there would be very little history written in the American academy. The diversity of thought and value permitted, and even stimulated, by our liberal polity has, as a natural consequence, the legitimation of pluralism in our universities.

A qualification must be added. By no means is every item of particularist learning academically acceptable. One way in which that is the case is that the things a person values and believes on account of some aspect of her character-identity may be things she is not *entitled* to value or believe—things she *should not* value or believe. The necessary qualification then is this: the scholar must be *entitled* to those particularist values and beliefs that shape her scholarship—as, indeed, she must be entitled to her nonparticularist values and beliefs. If her field is twenty-first-century American politics, she is not entitled to base her views exclusively on what she hears on her favorite news channel; she is obligated to read and listen more broadly.

But let us be cognizant of the fact that one person's entitled value or belief may contradict another person's entitled value or belief. Entitlement is, in that way, a situated phenomenon, unlike knowledge. If you believe P and I believe not-P, then at least one of us does not *know* P. Each of us may, however, be *entitled* to our belief.[11]

The Formation of Distinct Cognitive Natures

I have come to the end of my story. The explicit acceptance of particularity in the academy is, quite obviously, of wide-ranging import. Let me bring this chapter to a conclusion by highlighting what I see as one of the most important aspects of its import.

Recall Gadamer's claim that induction into a cultural tradition functions as *enabling* cognitive access to a certain dimension of reality. The person inducted into the Western cultural tradition thereby enjoys privileged cognitive access to what is said in the texts of the tradition. I suggest that the explicitly particularist scholarship produced over the past forty or fifty years points to the conclusion that something similar has to be said about some, at least, of our character-identities: certain aspects of a person's character-identity typically give her privileged cognitive access to certain dimensions of reality. Female scholars have called attention to dimensions of literature that male scholars overlooked. African American scholars have called attention to aspects of social reality that white scholars overlooked. And so forth.

It's important to add that by "privileged" access I do not mean *indispensable*. Overlooked aspects of literature that female scholars call to attention can usually also be discerned by male scholars, once those aspects are called to their attention—and once they are liberated from whatever resistances they may have. One sometimes hears members of a victimized group claim that only those who share their suffering can understand them—so there's no point in their talking to others. That may be true for understanding the suffering itself; suffering is highly individual. Suffering isolates. But if one's suffering gives one insight into some dimension of literature overlooked by others, usually, so it appears to me, that insight can be conveyed to others.

How does privileged cognitive access work? Let me approach my suggestion as to how it works by introducing Gadamer's memorable term, "homogeneous human nature." Contrary to the understanding of interpretation that he attributed to Schleirmacher, Gadamer argued that, in our interpretation of texts, we do not and cannot just employ our homogeneous human nature. Let me explain what I think he probably had in mind.

Among the innate belief-forming dispositions that we human beings possess, in addition to those of perception, introspection, and rational intuition, is what the great eighteenth-century Scots philosopher Thomas Reid called the "credulity" disposition: the disposition to believe, on their say-so, what people tell us. Induction into a tradition includes, among other things, coming to believe things on the say-so of members of the tradition, the underlying mechanism being that their assertions activate one's innate credulity disposition.

Gadamer was thinking, so I suggest, that by virtue of the workings of our credulity disposition, induction into a cultural tradition stocks one's mind with the "prejudgments" that enable one to interpret texts from the tradition. We pick up a text from our tradition with various prejudgments we have acquired, on the say-so of others, as to what it will say; we read, and our reading evokes in us beliefs as to what the text does in fact say. In case there is conflict between our prejudgments and what we now believe, either we read again or we replace those prejudgments with others we may have. And so it goes, back and forth, until we feel confident that we have understood the text.

When Gadamer argued that interpreting texts cannot be understood as a case of employing our homogeneous human nature, he was not arguing that we do not employ a shared human nature when we interpret; he was arguing that possessing and employing that nature is not sufficient for ordinary interpretation. We also need beliefs of a certain sort—prejudgments.

I now suggest that to explain how it is that certain of our character-identities give us privileged cognitive access to certain dimensions of reality, we have to go beyond Gadamer. A good many feminist studies point to the conclusion that women are characteristically disposed to notice certain things that men do not typically notice, and to form certain beliefs in certain situations that men are typically not disposed to form in those situations. They characteristically have different noticing selves and different belief-forming selves than men have.

Whether this is innate or the result of social formation is an issue we need not enter. So too, those living on the underside of society are often alert to aspects of reality that typically go unnoticed by those who possess power, and those who are gay or lesbian are often alert to aspects of reality that typically go unnoticed by those who are straight.

In short, what we learn from the recognition of particularities in the academy is that we, who are scholars, engage in our disciplines not only with partially different storehouses of beliefs but also with partially different cognitive dispositions—different *cognitive natures*, if you will.[12] We have all heard the suggestion that there are women's ways of knowing. Note well: not *things* women know, but women's *ways of knowing*. I think the conclusion to be drawn from the many fine feminist studies produced over the past half century is that the suggestion is true. Of course, if there are women's ways of knowing, then it seems likely that there are also men's ways of knowing.

It has been my experience that many people find this idea, when presented to them, troublesome. Yes, the person with eyesight more acute than average has privileged cognitive access to the visual world. But the idea that possessing a certain character-identity gives one privileged cognitive access to some dimension of reality: they find that idea deeply problematic.

But before the idea is dismissed, let us note that a similar idea has been around a long time. I am thinking of David Hume's analysis of what accounts for the formation of inductive beliefs about the future. Hume argued that we do not form such beliefs by valid inference from perceptual and introspective beliefs, nor *could* we so form them if we wanted. Rather, our experience of regular conjunctions among types of events produces in us the disposition, upon subsequently observing an event of one of those types, to believe that an event of the other type will be forthcoming. Having often seen the release of an object followed by its descent, a brand-new belief-disposition has been formed in me, so that now, upon seeing an object released, I believe it will descend. I have become a different belief-forming self from what I was before. We need those acquired inductive-belief dispositions—*habits*, Hume called them—if we are to have cognitive access to facts about the future. Our innate reality-accessing faculties and dispositions of perception, introspection, and rational intuition will not get us there.

There are important differences between the dispositions on which Hume focused, namely, our experientially acquired dispositions to form inductive beliefs about the future, and those to which I have been calling attention, namely, those dispositions that come along with certain of our character-identities. Hume argued that we cannot form inductive beliefs about the future without the formation of such dispositions. I have suggested that those aspects of reality which our character-identities dispose us to notice can usually also be discerned by those who lack that particular character-identity and that disposition—once those aspects of reality are called to their attention.

Let me close these reflections on the import of the explicit particularizing of the academy by taking a long step back in history. Augustine was already thinking along the lines I have been suggesting. Recall his apothegm, borrowed from Clement of Alexandria: *credo ut intelligam,* "I believe so that I may know." Belief is the condition of knowledge, knowledge is the goal of belief. The belief and knowledge Augustine had in mind were belief about God and knowledge of God. A condition of knowing God is that one have faith in God, faith understood by Augustine as consisting, in its core, of loving God. Only the person whose self is thus formed can come to know God, said Augustine. The argumentation is best laid out in his little book, *Of True Religion.*

REASSURANCE—OF SORTS

Some readers may have found Weber's argument presented in the preceding chapter depressing; it's likely that even more will have found the story told in this chapter somewhat dizzying. It resembles the opening fifty pages of a Tolstoy novel: almost impossible on first reading to keep all the characters straight. If that has been your experience, be assured that however complicated the philosophical moves may have seemed, the overarching story line itself is simple: we can no longer think in the old Weberian way about what transpires in the university. We have to think in new ways. Scholarship does not consist, and cannot consist, of just taking in the facts. Always we ourselves have to bring something to the table: values of various sorts, judgments of significance, theoretical preferences, prejudgments.

There may be other readers who are not so much dizzied as disturbed. They understand well enough the story I have been telling, and are disturbed by what seems to them the picture that emerges of an academy afloat on an ocean of subjectivity. In my final chapter I will say some things to alleviate this alarm. Not enough for some, I realize; they want proof. It is my conviction that at the bottom of our human existence there is, and must be, trust, not proof. It was an illusion to have thought otherwise.[13]

3
Rethinking Religion

Weber's analysis of the workings of the differentiated spheres in a modernized society led him to his claim that nonconforming religion has no place in the modern university. Others have argued that there is something about religion itself, not simply nonconforming religion, that makes it unfit for inclusion in the university. The argument most commonly offered for this position, and also the one that, in my judgment, is the most deserving of serious consideration, is that religion ought to be excluded from the university because it is not rational.[1] The social theorist Seyla Benhabib is reported as saying that religious people "suffer from a rationality deficit."[2]

"Rationality" is an ambiguous term, as is its companion term "reason." What might someone who says that religious people suffer from a rationality deficit mean by the term "rationality"? Most likely she has in mind our capacity for *reasoning*, that is, our capacity for devising, employing, and understanding *reasons* and for judging which are good ones and which are not. And by a "deficit" in rationality she most likely has in mind a malfunction or misuse of one's capacity for reasoning.

One's capacity for reasoning is *malfunctioning* if it is impaired in its workings; perhaps one has had a concussion, or a stroke, with the result that one can no longer reason as one once could. One's capacity for reasoning is not being *used properly* if one is not employing it as one should; one makes hasty generalizations, leaps to conclusions, and the like.[3]

Let's call beliefs that are indicative of one's reason malfunctioning or not being used properly, *nonrational* beliefs. And let's say that a belief is *rational* if, in how the belief is formed and maintained, there is no flaw in the functioning or use of one's capacity for reasoning.

Religions, as we all know, are highly diverse phenomena—*orientations* I called them in my opening chapter. They incorporate, among other things, ritual practices, moral commitments, and comprehensive worldviews, these last including both beliefs about the supramundane—the transcendent—and beliefs about the mundane, the former not just added to the latter but integrated with them, just as the rival metaphysical views of, say, a materialist are not just added to his views about the mundane but integrated with them into a comprehensive materialist worldview.

Critics of the sort I have in mind in this chapter have their eye on beliefs about the transcendent. They realize, no doubt, that there is more to religion than beliefs, and many of them realize that the beliefs of religious people about the supramundane are integrated with their beliefs about the mundane into comprehensive worldviews. But in the religions familiar to them— Judaism, Christianity, and Islam—beliefs about the transcendent are central. So they focus on those. In holding those beliefs, so the critic claims, the religious person's capacity for reasoning is either malfunctioning or not being used properly. For our purposes in this chapter, let's call beliefs about the transcendent "religious beliefs" —all the while keeping in mind that to focus on such beliefs is to abstract them from the religious worldviews in which they play a determinative role.

Nonrational beliefs, religious or not, have no place in the university, says the critic. We can tolerate—we have to tolerate—some measure of nonrational beliefs in everyday life. But given the role-ethic of the scholar, nonrational beliefs should play no role in a person's scholarship. In scholarship, properly conducted, there is no rationality deficit.

Some have argued, in recent years, that once the university allows within it distinct feminist voices, distinct African American voices, distinct Third World voices, distinct gay voices, and the like, then it cannot, with justice, exclude distinct religious voices.[4] To my mind, the argument has merit. But the person who regards religious beliefs as nonrational is not likely to find the argument persuasive. Feminism, she will say, is a rational perspective. Of course, it sometimes comes in excessive, irrational forms; but, as such, it is rational. Feminist literary critics have reasons for their views, they offer those reasons to others, and they entertain reasons offered by others against their views. And while being a woman may give one privileged cognitive access, in the process of discovery, to certain dimensions of reality, it is not a privilege of the sort that prevents others from noticing and believing the same things. In a spirit of good will, others can listen to what feminists say and have their eyes and minds opened. Religion, says the critic, is fundamentally different.

My focus in this chapter will be on the charge that religious beliefs are not rational and should, for that reason, be kept out of the academy. But it's worth noting parenthetically that critics attribute other epistemological deficiencies to religious beliefs that also make them unfit, so the critics insist, for inclusion in the academy.

Prominent in the lives of many religious people, especially those who are members of one of the Abrahamic religions, is believing so-and-so on the basis of an experience that the person interpreted as God saying or revealing so-and-so, or believing something on the basis of someone else's report of such an experience. These experiences are of many different sorts, and the role they play in the lives of religious persons and communities is likewise diverse. Compare, for example, Moses' conviction that God spoke to him on Mount Sinai, Saint Anthony's conviction that God spoke to him when he happened to overhear the reading of a passage from the New Testament, and Martin Luther King Jr.'s conviction that God spoke to him at breakfast one morning.

All beliefs based directly or indirectly on some purported revelatory experience must be kept out of the academy, says the critic; the differences make no difference. Of course, they must be kept out because they are, says the critic, nonrational. But what additionally makes them inadmissible is that they are *inaccessible* to all but the recipient of the purported revelation and that they are *immunized* against critique.

Those who make the claim of inaccessibility appear to have the following in mind. If I believe that there is a wild turkey in our garden because I see it, you can access that same fact in the same way I did: you can look out the window and employ your powers of visual perception. Or if you cannot look out the window because you are, say, a hundred miles away, accessing that same fact in the same way I did is something that you, possessing the same powers of visual perception that I possess, *could have* done.

Back, now, to the person who believes something because she is convinced that God revealed that to her. Suppose she has had an experience that she interpreted as God telling her that evolution is a divinely guided process. There is nothing the rest of us can do, notes the critic, to access, in the same way she did, the purported fact that evolution is a divinely guided process. There is nothing we can do to get God to reveal that to us— nothing we can do to get God to give us the experience of God telling us that evolution is a divinely guided process. For that reason, her belief has no place in the academy. In the academy, what one claims to be a fact has to be accessible, at least in principle, to one's fellow scholars in the same way that it is to oneself. No private revelations.

Further, says the critic, if a person believes so-and-so because she interprets an experience she had as God revealing that to her, she will likely not entertain arguments against the truth of so-and-so—not as long as she continues to believe firmly that God revealed it to her. She will *immunize* her belief against critique. But it is incompatible with the ethic of the scholar in the modern university, says the critic, to immunize any belief whatsoever against critique.

In the course of our discussion in this chapter and the next I will have something to say about the charge that religious beliefs are inaccessible and immunized. But my main focus, to repeat, will be on the charge that religious beliefs are not, in general, rational.

Over the past three or four decades, philosophers of religion have addressed the charge that religious belief is not rational far more creatively and extensively than ever before. Old lines of thought have been formulated with increased sophistication, and new ways of thinking about the rationality of religious beliefs have emerged, along with new ways of thinking about the rationality of beliefs in general. It is my judgment that any serious and informed discussion of the place of religion in the university must take these developments into account. Not only must we think anew about the nature of scholarship; we must also think anew about the rationality of religious beliefs. That is what we will do in the remainder of this chapter, employing the recent literature in philosophy of religion to do so. We will encounter some twists and turns; but I trust that those will not obscure the main lines of thought.

Most professors and students currently working in colleges and universities are aware of the developments I traced in the preceding chapter; it is my impression that relatively few are aware of the developments whose highlights I will now present. Most of them have heard, or heard about, the noisy fulminations of the so-called *new atheists*: Richard Dawkins, Daniel Dennett, Sam Harris, and Christopher Hitchens. But most of them know nothing of the vastly more sophisticated discussions by philosophers about the rationality of religious belief that I will now be referring to.

RELIGIOUS BELIEFS AND ARGUMENTS

What is it about the beliefs of religious people concerning the transcendent that the critic takes as indicative of the malfunctioning or misuse of their capacity for reasoning? Usually it's the fact that religious people typically do not hold their beliefs about the transcendent on the basis of arguments, let alone arguments that adequately support those beliefs. They hold them on faith, of one sort or another, and therein lies the deficiency in rationality, says the critic. Worse yet: often there are good arguments *against* their beliefs. Some theists believe, for example, that God created the world six thousand years ago, in spite of the fact that science has established that the earth is billions of years old. And many theists claim that God is omnipotent, omniscient, and all-good, in spite of the fact that this claim is defeated, so the critic says, by the nature and extent of evil in the world.

An internationally renowned German philosopher once remarked to me, "You are a fideist, are you not?" When I asked him what he meant by that, he said that he understood it to be my view that it was acceptable to hold my religious beliefs on faith rather than on the basis of arguments, and that I would probably not seriously entertain any arguments against them. "Fideist," for him, was not a term of praise!

I should explain that I use the term "argument" in the way that philosophers typically use the term, not in the way it is used in ordinary speech, where it is a synonym for "dispute." To say that someone holds a belief on the basis of an *argument* for the belief is to say that she holds it on the basis of something else she believes that she judges to support the belief—to provide evidence for it. Suppose, for example, that I believe that a rabbit was in our backyard last night on the basis of my belief that these tracks in the snow are characteristic of rabbits. That's an example of believing something on the basis of an argument. If the argument on the basis of which one holds a belief does in fact support the belief, I will say that it is *propositional evidence* for the belief.[5] And I will say that a belief not held on the basis of an argument is held *immediately*—the idea being that it is not "mediated" by other things one believes on which it is based. For example, when seeing a rabbit in my backyard, I immediately believe (without recourse to any argument) that there is a rabbit in my backyard.

Of course, religious people do sometimes hold their

religious beliefs on the basis of arguments. They hold a certain belief about the transcendent on the basis of another belief about the transcendent, and that one on the basis of yet another, and so on. That is true, for example, of the rather complicated beliefs of Christians about the Trinity and the Incarnation. Presumably the critic knows this. The phenomenon on which she has her eye is that religious people typically do not hold their religious beliefs *as a whole* on the basis of arguments whose premises lie *outside* the system of their religious beliefs; their arguments, when they do employ arguments, are usually from one part of the system to another part of the system.[6]

MEETING THE CHARGE
OF NONRATIONALITY

The critic is right in noting that many of the beliefs of religious people about the transcendent are not held on the basis of arguments. And as for those that are held on the basis of arguments, the premises of the arguments are often internal to their religious belief system. So how might the religious person respond to the charge that, in believing in this way, his capacity for reasoning is malfunctioning or not being used properly?

There are, in principle, two ways of responding. He might *meet* the charge, by developing good arguments and believing on the basis of those, thus satisfying the criterion for the rationality of religious belief that the critic employs, or he might *challenge* the charge, by arguing that the criterion for rationality that the critic employs is mistaken. Both ways of responding have been developed with great sophistication in the recent philosophy of religion literature. I propose spending most of my time on the second way of responding, since it represents a distinctly new way of thinking, whereas the heart of the first way of responding consists of continuing a line of thought that goes back millennia. But let's begin with the first way.

Over the centuries, back into antiquity, philosophers and religious thinkers have developed arguments for their core religious beliefs whose premises were not internal to their religious belief system. They have written books and delivered lectures in which they presented arguments of this sort for the existence and nature of God, arguments for the resurrection of Jesus from the dead, and so forth. The enterprise of developing such arguments is commonly called "natural theology."

In the nineteenth century, such arguments occupied a prominent place in the curricula of American colleges, most of which were Christian at the time. It was common for seniors to be required to take a capstone course, often taught by the president of the college, in which the instructor first argued that design in nature provides the key premise of an argument for the existence and nature of God, then argued that various events in history, coupled with certain features of Christian scripture, provide the premises of an argument for the conclusion that what Christian scripture reports as having transpired in ancient Israel and in the lives of Jesus and his followers is accurate, and then concluded by looking inside those scriptures for the personal and social ethic to be found therein. By now, such courses are a thing of the past, remembered only by a few historians.

Developing natural theological arguments for religious belief has by no means come to a halt, however. In recent decades, the endeavor has flourished as never before. Philosophers have reformulated the traditional arguments for God's existence and nature with extraordinary sophistication and have introduced a number of new arguments. Two excellent examples of the genre are

Alvin Plantinga's reformulation of Anselm's so-called ontological argument, employing new developments in modal logic,[7] and Richard Swinburne's reformulation of traditional so-called cosmological arguments, employing modern developments in probability theory (Bayesian theory).[8] By the present-day standards of the guild of philosophers, these are highly competent arguments; their authors hold prominent positions in the academy.[9]

It is my impression that most of those who charge religious people with suffering from a rationality deficit are either unaware of this sophisticated body of thought or have not worked through it with care and an open mind.[10] Careful analysis and criticism of present-day formulations of the theistic arguments come, for the most part, from those who are themselves religious, not from those who are not. There is no mystery in that. Most of those who charge religious people with suffering from a rationality deficit are resistant to acknowledging the existence of God; it's not a possibility they are willing to entertain. If that is one's attitude, why immerse oneself in a careful study of the theistic arguments? Best to either ignore them or dismiss them out of hand.

Bringing Testimony into the Picture

The existence of this impressive body of thought means that the condition laid down by the critic for the inclusion of one's religious voice in the academy has been met—met by those who have studied the theistic arguments and found them persuasive. They now hold their core religious beliefs on the basis of arguments whose premises come from outside their religious belief system. It's likely that most of them held those beliefs before they studied the arguments; for most of them, the arguments function as articulating certain "gut intuitions" that they had well before they studied the arguments.[11] But whether or not they held those beliefs before they studied the arguments, now they hold them on the basis of the arguments—though perhaps not *just* on the basis of the arguments. They have met the challenge of the critic. Their religious voice has a place in the university!

But most religious people have not studied the arguments—and that includes most religious people who are members of university faculties: members of English departments, of history departments, of sociology departments. They may have heard about the theistic arguments, but most of them have not studied them, and so, of course, they don't hold their religious beliefs on the basis of the arguments. The critic's point was not that there are no supporting arguments for religious belief—though probably most of those who regard religious believers as suffering from a rationality deficit do believe that. The critic's point was that, whether or not there are such arguments, most religious people do not *hold* their religious beliefs *on the basis of* arguments whose premises lie outside their religious belief system. Therein, says the critic, lies the deficiency in rationality.

May it be, however, that the critic has too narrow a view of how the existence of arguments for a certain belief contributes to the rationality of that belief? The critic tacitly assumes that one has to hold the belief on the basis of the arguments for the arguments to contribute to the belief's rationality. But may it be that there is another way of being related to the arguments that also contributes to the rationality of the belief? May it be that even though one is not acquainted with the theistic arguments, and hence does not hold one's religious beliefs on the basis of those arguments, nonetheless, the existence of those arguments does contribute, in a certain way, to the rationality of one's beliefs?

Consider the fact that though all laypeople in modernized societies hold beliefs established by modern natural science, they do not hold them in the way scientists hold them, namely, on the basis of arguments that support those beliefs. Holding them in that way is inaccessible to laypeople—as inaccessible as holding a belief in the way someone does who says God revealed it to her.[12] Laypeople hold their beliefs about the results of the natural sciences on the basis of testimony.[13]

I read a text in physics and believe what I read because I assume the author "knows his stuff"; I listen to an astronomy lecture and believe what the lecturer says because I've been told he's an expert in the field. Nobody regards my holding scientific beliefs in this way as a breakdown in the functioning or proper use of my capacity for reasoning. Why not extend the same courtesy to my religious beliefs? Why not think about the rationality of religious belief along similarly communitarian rather than individualistic lines? Why not hold that the proper use or functioning by religious people of their capacity for reasoning requires not that each and every individual believe on the basis of arguments of the requisite sort but that, within the community, there be arguments of that sort, and that members of the community who are not directly acquainted with those arguments be related by reliable chains of testimony to those who are directly acquainted?[14]

I imagine a response: there is a significant difference between the scientific community and the religious community on this matter of testimony. Whereas there is usually substantial agreement among natural scientists working in some particular field of inquiry, which is why it is acceptable for the rest of us to believe on their say-so what they tell us about the results in their field, there is nothing comparable in the religious community.[15]

But there *is* something comparable in the religious community. As I noted above, there is substantial agreement among those philosophers working in the area of natural theology on the cogency of various arguments for the existence and nature of God—not complete agreement, indeed, but substantial. It's that substantial agreement that makes it acceptable for those religious people who are not philosophers to believe what philosophers tell them when they report that there are cogent natural theological arguments for the existence and nature of God. Doing so does not represent a malfunction or misuse of their capacity for reasoning.

It's true, of course, as I noted above, that those philosophers who are resistant to acknowledging the existence of God usually either ignore these arguments or dismiss them out of hand. Is that relevant? I think not. Consider the science of climate change. Scientists who work in the area report that there is a very high level of agreement among them on the facts of climate change, its causes, and its effects. That's why I accept on their say-so what they tell me. But I realize that there are also some people, trained in science, who are deniers of climate change. Though some of these hold university positions, most of them work for organizations that have a stake in either denying climate change or denying that human activity has much to do with it. The existence of those deniers does not make it unacceptable for me to believe what the great majority of scientists who work in the area tell me.

We are touching here on an underdeveloped area

in philosophy generally, and in philosophy of religion in particular, namely, the epistemology of testimony. Testimony, and acceptance of testimony, pervade the lives of all of us; accepting the testimony of scientists on topics in their field of specialty constitutes only a tiny part of what any of us accepts on testimony. So, too, testimony and the acceptance of testimony are prominent in religion. Yet, until very recently, philosophers in general, and philosophers of religion in particular, have paid almost no attention to the epistemology of testimony.[16] I understand the reason for this neglect. Epistemology of the modern period has been shaped by the image of human beings as solitary individuals forming beliefs by perception, introspection, rational intuition, inference, memory, and so on. But testimony, and the acceptance of testimony, are inherently communal in character.

After long neglect, the epistemology of testimony in general is now a rapidly developing field of inquiry, the seminal book in the area being C. A. J. Coady's *Testimony: A Philosophical Study*.[17] I predict that the role of testimony in religion, and the epistemology of holding religious beliefs on the basis of testimony, will also soon take off.[18]

Challenging the Charge
of Nonrationality

I noted that there are, in principle, two ways in which the religious person might respond to the charge that he suffers from a rationality deficit on account of not holding his religious beliefs on the basis of arguments that adequately support those beliefs: he might *meet* the charge, by developing such arguments, or he might *challenge* the charge, by arguing that the criterion the critic employs for assessing religious beliefs as nonrational is mistaken. And I mentioned that both ways of responding have been developed with great sophistication in recent years by philosophers of religion. Having summarized recent developments in the first way of responding, let me now turn to recent developments in the second way of responding.

Beginning some forty years ago, philosophers of religion have asked whether it's true, as the critic assumes, that not holding one's religious beliefs on the basis of arguments that adequately support those beliefs represents a deficiency in the functioning or use of one's capacity for reasoning. What reason is there for contending that believing something *immediately* about God or the afterlife perforce indicates a deficit in rationality? Be it granted that sometimes it does. But always and everywhere? Why?[19] (It would be several decades before philosophers fully realized the relevance of testimony to this question.)

Those who challenged the demand for propositional evidence pointed to the fact that we all hold many beliefs immediately without anybody taking that to be a deficiency of rationality on our part. So why insist that holding *religious* beliefs immediately always and everywhere indicates a deficiency of rationality? What is it about religious beliefs that makes them different?

It has been my experience that many people are taken aback by the claim that we all hold many beliefs immediately. Something in their socialization has led them to assume that all beliefs are held on the basis of other beliefs—on the basis of arguments. Often we're not conscious of the argument. But supposedly it's there, in the background.

It takes just a bit of reflection to see that that cannot be how it is. It's impossible to hold all of one's beliefs on the basis of other beliefs. I can believe A on the basis of B and B on the basis of C and C on the basis of D, and so forth. But somewhere the chain has to end—or better, begin. It can't go on forever, and it can't go in circles. The mental activity of *believing something on the basis of something else one believes* cannot be the sole mode of belief-formation. There have to be other modes of belief-formation that produce beliefs on which that activity can do its work. There have to be some modes of belief-formation that produce beliefs *immediately*—without the "mediation" of other things one believes. The term commonly used in the literature is "properly basic." One must have some beliefs that are properly basic.[20]

Examples of beliefs that are held immediately, and properly so, are easy to come by. When I believe that I feel dizzy, I don't believe that on the basis of an argument. What would an argument for this belief look like? But surely it's okay to believe this immediately; no rationality deficit. So, too, for my belief that I see a wild turkey in our garden and for my belief that 1+1=2. I don't believe either of these on the basis of an argument. I believe them immediately, and nobody regards me as suffering from a rationality deficit on that account.[21]

This all seems obvious once the point is made. But why, then, hold that *religious* beliefs, to be rational, must be held on the basis of arguments? What makes religious beliefs, in general, different in this respect from perceptual, introspective, and rational intuitive beliefs? What is the relevant difference? In their original essays, those who asked this question found no plausible answer.[22]

The claim that religious beliefs must be held on the basis of arguments to be rational was tabbed "evidentialism" with respect to religious beliefs. The line of thought that was emerging was described as "anti-evidentialism." But after some time, a number of participants in the discussion began questioning the way in which the terms "evidentialism" and "anti-evidentialism" were being used. It was misleading, they said, to characterize the positions in dispute as "evidentialism" and "anti-evidentialism." Their reason for making that claim opened up new areas to be explored. But before we get to that, I propose taking a step back in history.

LOCKE'S REASON FOR HOLDING THAT RELIGIOUS BELIEFS MUST BE BASED ON ARGUMENTS

To the best of my knowledge, it was the seventeenth-century English philosopher John Locke who first articulately propounded and defended the thesis that, for religious beliefs to be rational, they must be held on the basis of arguments—arguments of a quite specific sort, let me add. In his defense of this thesis, he pointed out what it was about religious beliefs that, in his judgment, made arguments necessary, whereas they are not necessary for perceptual, introspective, and rational intuitive beliefs. Though Locke's account of the relevant difference does not, in the final account, hold up, I think it will prove illuminating to see what he said. My guess is that certain aspects of his account remain influential in how many people think about these matters.

Locke did not actually use the term "rational" in this connection. What he said was that, for religious beliefs to be held *responsibly*, they must be held on the basis of arguments of a certain sort. But his thought was that failure to hold one's religious beliefs on the basis of such arguments constitutes a misuse of one's capacity for reasoning, so we do not distort his thought if we describe him as holding that a condition of holding one's religious beliefs rationally is that one hold them on the basis of arguments that support those beliefs. Here is a passage from his *Essay Concerning Human Understand-*

ing in which he states his position with great force and eloquence:

> However faith be opposed to reason, faith is nothing but a firm assent of the mind; which if it be regulated, as is our duty, cannot be afforded to anything but upon good reason, and so cannot be opposite to it. He that believes, without having any reason for believing, may be in love with his own fancies; but neither seeks truth as he ought, nor pays the obedience due to his Maker, who would have him use those discerning faculties he has given him, to keep him out of mistake and error. . . . For he governs his assent right, and places it as he should, who, in any case or matter whatsoever, believes or disbelieves according as reason directs him. He that does otherwise, transgresses against his own light, and misuses those faculties which were given him to no other end, but to search and follow the clearer evidence and greater probability. (IV.17.24)

Medieval philosopher-theologians, such as Anselm and Aquinas, held that theology has to be rationally grounded on arguments. What they had in mind by "theology" was the science of theology, the academic discipline, the *scientia*. Locke was not talking about the academic discipline of theology but about the religious beliefs of the ordinary person. Ordinary persons, not just professional theologians, must see to it that their religious beliefs are held on the basis of arguments.[23] That, he says, is their solemn duty.

Locke's thesis concerning the rationality of religious belief was a direct implication of his general epistemology. So let's get in hand as much of his general epistemology as is necessary to understand his thought in the passage quoted.[24]

Consider some proposition that, for one reason or another, has become a candidate for belief on your part. Now suppose that the proposition is not immediately certain for you, and that you want to do your human best to believe it if and only if it is true. What should you do?

Locke's answer, elegant in its simplicity, went as follows. You should begin by looking around for evidence for and against the truth of the proposition, and you should accept something as evidence only if it is certain for you; anything less than that would not be doing the best. You should continue collecting evidence until your sample is sufficiently ample, and until it is representative of all the evidence on the matter that there is; you should not be satisfied with just a bit of evidence, and you should not look just for confirming or just for disconfirming evidence. When you finally have such a body of evidence in hand, you should look it over to see how probable is the proposition in question on that evidence. Once you arrive at an answer to that question, you should proceed to believe or disbelieve the proposition with a firmness proportioned to its probability on the evidence. If the probability of the truth of the proposition on the evidence is very high, you should believe it very firmly; if the probability of its truth is very low, you should disbelieve it very firmly. And so forth. This is the best a human being can do when the proposition in question is not itself immediately certain; nobody can do better than this.

It sounds exhausting and time-consuming. Locke agreed that it is. He held, accordingly, that each of us can employ the method for only a relatively few propositions; the universalistic tone struck by the passage I quoted is seriously misleading in that respect.

So when is a person supposed to employ the method? That depends, in good measure, on one's vocation and, more generally, on the particular contour of one's duties. One's duties make certain things of "maximal concernment" for one; it is on such matters that one is obligated to employ the method. For example, it is of maximal concernment for nurses that they dispense the right medicines to their patients; so that's when they should employ the method. It was Locke's view that it is of maximal concernment for each of us that we get things right on matters of ethics and religion. On such matters, we must all employ the method.[25]

One point of exposition remains. What did Locke take to be certain? There is a bit of wavering in what he says on the matter. But I think the evidence points to the conclusion that, on his view, the only faculties that yield full certitude are rational intuition and introspection. My belief that 1+1=2 is certain for me when I have the experience of "seeing" that it is true; so too, my belief that I feel dizzy is certain for me when I have the experience of feeling dizzy.

What about perceptual beliefs? Those, according to Locke, are not certain. My belief that it *appears* to me that I am seeing a wild turkey in our garden is certain for me; it's a report of my inner experience. But my belief that I am *actually seeing* a wild turkey in our garden is not certain for me; it's a claim not only about my experience but also about the world, and it might just possibly be false. Many of our perceptual beliefs are false. They are not certain for us.

Locke's epistemology of religious beliefs follows straightforwardly from his general epistemology, plus his claim that matters of morality and religion are always of maximal concernment for everyone. One's religious beliefs are not certain for one. They do not have, as their propositional content, either states of one's self that one can introspect or necessary truths that one can rationally intuit. So, given that getting things right on matters of religion is of maximal concernment for each of us, it is our duty to employ the Lockean method for our religious beliefs.

Religion, Locke claimed, is of "maximal concernment"; accordingly, religious beliefs, unlike beliefs about rabbits and turkeys, require the support of arguments. I think we can hear echoes of this Lockean claim in the words of those who charge religious believers with suffering from a rationality deficit. Of course, they don't have anything so sophisticated in mind as Locke's epistemology. They are thinking more intuitively. Nonetheless, my guess is that in the back of their minds there is the unarticulated conviction, shared with Locke, that since human destiny and the existence and nature of God are matters of deep importance, we should all do our best to get it right on such matters.

WHY LOCKE'S SUGGESTION HAS TO BE REJECTED

Is Locke's case compelling, for the thesis that religious beliefs, to be rational, must be held on the basis of arguments of the sort he identifies? It is not. Locke's argument is complex, and susceptible to critique at several points. Let me confine myself to a point that can be made quickly and that, so it seems to me, is decisive.

For the past three centuries, philosophers have tried to construct "proofs of the existence of the external world" of exactly the sort that Locke delineates: proofs whose premises consist exclusively of beliefs about inner experience and beliefs whose propositional content consists of some necessary truth that one "sees" to be true. The news from the trenches is that all those attempts have failed.[26] Philosophers who are still trying to prove the existence of an external world are an endangered species, if not extinct.

Now recall the example I gave of a matter of maximal concernment. It's a matter of maximal concernment for a nurse that she dispense the right medicines to her patients. Given that no one has succeeded in constructing a proof of the external world of a Lockean sort, it follows that she cannot employ any of her perceptual beliefs about the world in determining which are the right medicines. But if she cannot employ her perceptual beliefs, how can she determine which are the right medicines?

Clearly something is amiss in Locke's general epistemology. And it is on his general epistemology that he rested his claim that our religious beliefs, to be rational, must be held on the basis of arguments, whereas of many other beliefs, that is not the case.[27]

End of our detour into history.

EXPERIENTIAL AND TESTIMONIAL EVIDENCE

I mentioned that after the discussion concerning the necessity of arguments for one's religious belief had gone on for some time, a number of participants in the discussion began questioning the use of the terms "evidentialism" and "anti-evidentialism" to characterize what was in dispute. The terms were being employed in such a way as to characterize beliefs not held on the basis of arguments as beliefs not held on the basis of evidence. But that, they argued, was a mistake.

Consider, once again, my belief that I see a wild turkey in our garden. I don't hold this belief on the basis of an argument—that is, on the basis of other beliefs of mine from which I infer it. But neither does it just inexplicably lodge itself in my mind. My perceptual experience of seeing a wild turkey in our garden *evokes* the belief; I believe it *on the basis of* my perceptual experience. And not only does the experience evoke the belief in me; the experience is *evidence* for the belief—call it *experiential* evidence, in contrast to *propositional* evidence. Thomas Reid and other eighteenth-century writers called such evidence "evidence of the senses."

So too, my introspective experience of feeling dizzy both evokes in me the belief that I feel dizzy and constitutes experiential evidence for the belief, and my rational intuitive experience of "seeing" that 1+1=2 both evokes in me the belief that 1+1=2 and constitutes experiential evidence for the belief.

While we are on the topic of different kinds of evidence, let's also bring *testimonial* evidence into the picture. I don't believe that the earth is billions of years old on the basis of arguments. But neither do I just find myself believing it. I believe it on the basis of testimony by scientists, and that testimony is evidence for it. I have testimonial evidence for it.

Now apply these points to religious beliefs. When philosophers of religion, about forty years ago, first began challenging the claim that religious beliefs, to be rational, had to be held on the basis of propositional evidence—supporting arguments—it may well have been the case that the picture of religious beliefs evoked in the minds of some readers was a picture of religious beliefs as held on *no basis* and on *no evidence*. But that picture is wrong. Perhaps some religious people do hold some of their religious beliefs on no basis whatsoever; they just find themselves believing something about God or the afterlife. But that is certainly not true in general. What's typical of religious beliefs not held on the basis of arguments is that they are held on the basis of experience or testimony.

Sometimes the experience is a distinctly religious

experience, such as a mystical experience, or an experience interpreted as that of God revealing something to one. But often it is not a distinctly religious experience. Many people, when they focus on the immensity and intricacy of the natural world, find the conviction welling up within them that behind it all there has to be a being of incredible intelligence and power. So, too, many, when they focus on the fine-tuning of the laws of nature that is required to make life possible, or on the fit between our human cognitive capacities and the structure of things, find that conviction welling up in them. Recall Immanuel Kant's famous remark: "Two things fill the mind with ever new and increasing admiration and awe, the more often and steadily we reflect upon them: the starry heavens above me and the moral law within me."[28]

Do Experience and Testimony Constitute Evidence for Religious Beliefs?

I have just now spoken of religious believers as holding their beliefs *on the basis of* experience or testimony. I refrained from taking the next step of claiming that the experience or testimony constitutes *evidence for* the beliefs. But that, now, is the question that our line of thought about evidence places before us. Do experience and testimony sometimes constitute evidence for the religious beliefs they evoke? If they do not, but if religious beliefs do have to be held on the basis of evidence to be rational, then (assuming that there are no other types of evidence than those plus propositional evidence) the claim of the critic presented at the beginning of this chapter is true, namely, that religious beliefs, to be rational, must be held on the basis of propositional evidence. Not holding one's religious beliefs on the basis of propositional evidence represents a malformation or misuse of one's capacity for reasoning.

I see no reason to hold that experience and testimony never constitute good evidence for the religious beliefs they evoke. What reason could there be for making that bold universalized claim? It's true, of course, that sometimes the experience or testimony that evokes some religious belief does not constitute good evidence for the belief; but the same is true for beliefs based on perceptual experience or on testimony. In all these cases, one has to get down into the trenches and argue that point for the specific case at hand.

Often the content of a religious belief does not replicate the content of the experience that evoked it. Though my experience of meditating on the astounding intricacy of some aspect of reality evokes in me the conviction that behind it all there has to be a creator, the content of the belief does not replicate the content of the experience. Might that be a reason for regarding such religious beliefs as lacking in evidence?

But the same is true for many perceptual beliefs. My experience of hearing a certain sound coming from the direction of the street evokes in me the belief that a car is passing by; the content of the belief does not replicate the content of the experience but goes beyond it. Yet, surely, the experience is evidence for the belief. Or take an example that figured prominently in the thought of Thomas Reid, to whom I have already referred several times: one's experiencing a touch sensation of a certain sort evokes in one the belief that one is touching a hard object, but the content of the belief does not replicate the content of the experience. Yet the experience, surely, is evidence for the belief.

Let's try again. Might it be that although experience and testimony do often constitute evidence for the religious beliefs they evoke, they never constitute *sufficient* evidence for the belief to be fully rational? For the evidence to be sufficient, the beliefs must also be held on the basis of arguments that support them.

I see no more reason for holding this middle-of-the-road position on the bearing of experience and testimony on religious beliefs, namely, that they provide some evidence but never sufficient evidence, than for holding the extreme position, that they never provide any evidence.

A question lurking in the background that I have not addressed is whether religious beliefs do have to be held on the basis of evidence of some sort to be rational; I have confined myself to asking whether, as the critic insists, they have to be held on the basis of *propositional* evidence. Might it be the case that religious beliefs, in general, do not have to be held on the basis of anything that can plausibly be called "evidence" to be rational? The critic tacitly assumes they do. Is that assumption correct?

Though this is obviously the most fundamental question of all, it's impossible to address it in this essay. Let me just take note of a position that emerged in general epistemology in the early years of the twenty-first century that was called *evidentialism* by its original proponents, Earl Conee and Richard Feldman. "What we call evidentialism," they said, "is the view that the epistemic justification of a belief is determined by the quality of the believer's evidence for the belief."[29] Justification is not the same as rationality; but if this general thesis were true for justification, one would certainly want to consider whether it is also true for rationality.

The position has proved highly controversial. Disputes have broken out over what constitutes evidence, over what it is to believe something on the basis of evidence, and over when a body of evidence adequately supports a proposition. Even its original proponents have come to see their proposal as no more than "the bare sketch of a full theory of epistemic justification."[30]

Let me close this section of my discussion with two comments. First, I mentioned earlier that analysis of testimonial evidence in religion, as in life generally, is still in its infant stages. The analysis of experiential evidence in religion is somewhat more advanced. A seminal book in the area is William P. Alston's *Perceiving God*,[31] in which he analyzes various reports of mystical experience and argues that the experience constitutes evidence for the belief about God that it evokes.

Second, it is my conviction that each of us should ourselves be alert to reasons for thinking that some belief of ours is mistaken, be it perceptual, religious, or whatever, and not just wait for others to point that out to us. That, as I see it, is the proper use, in general, of one's capacity for reasoning. To speak epigrammatically: beliefs, in general, are innocent until proven guilty, not guilty until proven innocent.[32]

Reviewing Where We Are

At the end of the preceding chapter, I observed that it's likely some readers found themselves dizzied by the story I told there of recent developments in the understanding and practice of academic learning. It's likely that even more readers have found themselves dizzied by the story I have told in this chapter of recent developments in our understanding of the rationality of religious beliefs, even though I have only skimmed the surface. So before we draw this chapter to a close, let me briefly recapitulate the high points of the story.

We have been considering the claim that religion has no place in the university because religious beliefs are nonrational. They are, says the critic, indicative of a flaw in the functioning or use of one's capacity for reasoning. To be rational, they have to be held on the basis of arguments that support them and whose premises are not themselves religious beliefs. But typically they are not held on the basis of such arguments.

One way in which the religious person can respond to this charge of nonrationality is to meet the charge by developing the arguments called for and holding her beliefs on the basis of those arguments. I noted that, over millennia, philosophers and religious thinkers have done exactly that—they have developed natural theological arguments for religious beliefs, especially for the existence and nature of God—and I called attention to the fact that this project has gained momentum in recent decades with the development of new arguments and the formulation of old arguments with increased sophistication. Those who are acquainted with these arguments and now hold their religious beliefs, in part, at least, on the basis of such arguments, have met the condition the critic laid down for being allowed to employ one's religious beliefs in one's scholarship.

But most religious people are not acquainted with these theistic arguments, including many, if not most, scholars; and these people, obviously, do not hold their religious beliefs on the basis of such arguments. Does the resurgence of natural theology nonetheless have some relevance for them? Does it contribute, in some way, to the rationality of their beliefs?

It does. Those of us who are not scientists do not hold our scientific beliefs on the basis of arguments that provide propositional evidence for them. We hold them on the basis of testimony by those who do know the arguments; and nobody regards that as representing a malfunction or misuse of our capacity for reasoning. The same sort of thing is true for religious beliefs. The religious beliefs of those not acquainted with the theistic arguments gain rationality from being related by chains of testimony to those who are acquainted with the arguments.

The other way in which the religious person can respond to the charge that religious beliefs are nonrational because they are not held on the basis of natural theological arguments that support them is to challenge the charge. And that's what philosophers of religion have also done over the past forty years or so. What reason is there, they have asked, for thinking that the charge is true? They have called attention to the fact that all of us hold many beliefs immediately, that is, not on the basis of arguments—perceptual beliefs, introspective beliefs, rational intuitive beliefs—and nobody judges all such beliefs to represent a malformation or misuse of our capacity for reasoning. What's the relevant difference? Initially, no plausible suggestion as to a relevant difference was forthcoming.

Then a twist was introduced into the discussion. Some participants observed that it was being tacitly assumed that propositional evidence for beliefs is the only form of evidence. But the assumption is mistaken. Though perceptual beliefs are not held on the basis of propositional evidence, it doesn't follow that they are held on no evidence. When things go well, the perceptual experience that evokes the belief is evidence for the belief. So too for introspective beliefs and rational intuitive beliefs: when things go well, the experience that evokes the belief is evidence for the belief.

These observations about different types of evidence led to reframing the discussion about the rationality of religious beliefs. The critic is to be interpreted as claiming that religious beliefs have to be held on the basis of evidence and that experience and testimony never constitute evidence, or never *sufficient* evidence. Only propositional evidence is capable of providing sufficient evidence, and usually that is lacking. I noted that no one has come forward to offer a plausible defense of the bold claim that experience and testimony are never sufficient evidence for religious beliefs.[33]

In short: there is no reason to accept the claim that religious beliefs not held on the basis of natural theological arguments that adequately support them represent a malfunction or misuse of one's faculty of reasoning and that they should, for that reason, be kept out of the university.

An Alternative Interpretation of the Critique

Up to this point, I have focused on those critics who claim that religious beliefs are not rational because they are not held in the right way—not held on the basis of good arguments. Let me conclude my discussion in this chapter by considering the views of those who point to a quite different feature of religious beliefs that, purportedly, makes them inherently nonrational and hence unfit for inclusion in the academy. Whether or not religious people hold their beliefs in the right way, there is something about the *content* of their beliefs, so it is said, that represents a deficiency in rationality.

I have in mind those critics who interpret religious beliefs as theories functioning for the believer as *explanations* of one thing or another.[34] They believe in God because they think God's existence and action explain, for example, the origin of the universe, designlike features in the natural world, mystical experiences, moral obligation, and so on. The critic insists that all such explanations are unacceptable. Either the phenomenon in question doesn't need explanation—the Big Bang doesn't need explanation—or the religious explanation is a bad or inferior explanation. Designlike features in nature can be explained by evolution; no need to appeal to something so exotic and implausible as God.

In response to this critique, one can also go in either of two directions. One can challenge the claim or assumption that religious beliefs, in general, are theories that function for believers as explanations, or one can challenge the claim that religious beliefs, when understood as explanations, are uniformly bad or inferior explanations, and hence not rational. Both of these ways of responding have been developed in the recent literature on philosophy of religion.[35]

Already in the 1960s Ludwig Wittgenstein, in his remarks on religion in *Lectures and Conversations on Aesthetics, Psychology, and Religious Belief,*[36] challenged the interpretation of religious beliefs as explanations. He understood the anthropologist James Frazer, in his famous *The Golden Bough*, to be interpreting the religious beliefs of "primitive" people as crude explanations that have been replaced by the much better explanations of modern science, and he responded with fury: Frazer, wrote Wittgenstein, "is much more savage than most of his savages, for these savages will not be so far from any understanding of spiritual matters as an Englishman of the twentieth century. His explanations of the primitive observances are much cruder than the sense of the observances themselves."[37] Wittgenstein continues: "The doctrine of predestination simply isn't a theory."[38]

Wittgenstein's remarks on religion are scattered and epigrammatic. The philosopher who, in my judgment, has most powerfully argued the point that a good many religious beliefs do not function as explanations is William Alston in the book already mentioned, *Perceiving God.* As data for his analysis, Alston quotes some twenty-five reports of mystical experience. The first is representative of the group; Alston took it from William James's *Varieties of Religious Experience:*

> All at once I . . . felt the presence of God—I tell of the thing just as I was conscious of it—as if his goodness and his power were penetrating me altogether. . . . Then, slowly, the ecstasy left my heart. . . . I think it well to add that in this ecstasy of mine God had neither form, color, odor, nor taste; moreover, that the feeling of his presence was accompanied by no determinate localization. . . . But the more I seek words to express this intimate intercourse, the more I feel the impossibility of describing the thing by any of our images. At bottom the expression most apt to render what I felt is this: God was present, though invisible; he fell under no one of my senses, yet my consciousness perceived him.[39]

Alston notes, about this passage and the others like it that he quotes and analyzes, that the language is the language of perception, not the language of explanation. The person is describing his experience, not explaining it. It is open to the atheist to insist that the experience was illusory: the person did not experience the presence of God but only seemed to. But that, in any case, is how it seemed to him.[40] The beliefs his experience gave rise to were beliefs about his experience *as it seemed to him*, not beliefs that functioned for him as explanations of his experience.

The other response to the charge we are considering is to agree that, for at least some religious people, some of their religious beliefs do function as explanations, implicitly if not explicitly, and to challenge the assumption that those are bad or inferior explanations. Earlier I referred to the truly remarkable flowering, in recent years, of arguments for the existence and nature of God—new arguments, and newly formulated old arguments. Many of these arguments are in the form of explanations; that is true, for example, of the arguments that Richard Swinburne develops in *The Existence of God*.[41] Some of the theistic explanations that Swinburne and others offer are explanations of phenomena that the ordinary believer might well have taken note of and believed were explained by the existence and action of God—but developed with a sophistication well beyond the capacities of the ordinary person. Others are explanations of phenomena that the ordinary believer will never have noticed—the fine tuning of the cosmos, for example,[42] or the existence of abstract entities such as properties. Given this extraordinary development, it is now irresponsible to dismiss with a wave of the hand religious explanations as uniformly bad or inferior. Those who regard a particular explanation as bad or inferior will have to get down into the trenches and argue the case in detail.

In Conclusion

The developments I have traced, in the understanding of the rationality of religious belief that has emerged from the recent literature on the topic, could be presented in far greater detail than I have presented them here; I have only skimmed the surface.[43] But enough has been said to give us good reason to reject the blanket charge against religious beliefs, that they are nonrational and should, for that reason, be kept out of the university. In reflecting on the place of religion in the university, we must not only think anew about the nature of scholarship but also think anew about the rationality of religious belief. And about the nature of religion. We'll be getting to that in the next chapter.

Let me conclude this chapter by addressing a question that will have arisen in the minds of many readers. If we accept these new ways of thinking about the rationality of religious belief, must we conclude that anything goes by way of religious belief?

Not at all. Some religious beliefs do represent a malfunction or misuse of the person's capacity for reasoning. For example: suppose that, in retrospect, I see that I was gullible in taking Susan at her word when she told me about some purportedly religious experience she had; there were warning signs of schizophrenia that I should have paid attention to but did not. I did not employ my capacity for reasoning as I should have. I suffered from a rationality deficit—a *specific* deficit, a deficit *in this case*. So too, the person who believes, against the scientific evidence, that the earth is only six thousand years old because she believes those who claim that that's an implication of the biblical genealogies, is suffering from a specific rationality deficit.

The lesson to be drawn from our discussion is not that religious people do not suffer from a deficit in their rationality. They do, as do all human beings. They suffer from *specific cases* of deficiency. The lesson to be drawn from our discussion is that religious people do not suffer from some generalized deficiency of rationality just by virtue of holding religious beliefs. Or to state the upshot of our discussion more modestly: we have found no reason to think that religious beliefs, in general, represent a deficiency in rationality and should, for that reason, be kept out of the university.

The renowned American philosopher Richard Rorty, avowed atheist, wrote the following about religion and politics in his late essay "Religion as a Conversation Stopper." What he said about religion and politics applies to religion and scholarship as well. "The best parts of [Stephen Carter's] very thoughtful, and often persuasive, book [*The Culture of Disbelief*] are those in which he points up the inconsistency of our behavior, and the hypocrisy involved in saying that believers somehow have no right to base their political views on their religious faith, whereas we atheists have every right to base ours on Enlightenment philosophy. The claim that in doing so we are appealing to reason, whereas the religious are being irrational, is hokum. Carter is quite right to debunk it."[44]

✄ 4 ✄
Religion in the University

I n his book of prose reflections, *The Land of Ulro,* the Nobel prize–winning Lithuanian-Polish poet Czeslaw Milosz quotes a ballad entitled "The Romantic" by the nineteenth-century Polish poet Adam Mickiewicz. The ballad is about a village girl who, in agonized grief two years after the death of her beloved Johnny, has visions of his return. A crowd from the village assembles, joined in sympathy. Suddenly the intimation sweeps through the crowd that Johnny has come back from the grave. They cross themselves. The narrator prays. Then "a man with a learned air" shouts:

> The girl is out of her senses! . . .
> My eye and my lenses
> Know there's nothing there.
> . . . This is treason
> Against King Reason!

The narrator replies,

> Yet the girl loves,
> And the people believe reverently:
> Faith and love are more discerning
> Than lenses or learning.[1]

Faith and love versus lenses and learning. To choose for faith and love against lenses and learning is to commit treason against King Reason. It's the picture propounded with unparalleled depth, sweep, and melancholic passion by that great theorist of modernity, Max Weber.

The main burden of what I have to say in this book is that the choice is misconceived. Reasoning is fundamental to our existence; to be human is to reason. But though reason may often appear king in the realm of learning, close scrutiny shows that, in scholarship and teaching, our capacity for reasoning is always functioning in the service of some particular faith or love, or in the service of some intuition or interpretation of how things are.[2]

RECALLING OUR PREVIOUS DISCUSSION

Let's recall some of the high points of our discussion in the first two chapters. In Chapter 1, I discussed the understanding of scholarship on which there was widespread agreement in the first half of the twentieth century: when entering the academy, we are to put a lock on the storehouse of beliefs and values embedded within the religions we live by and the traditions into which we have been inducted, and make do with the deliverances of perception, introspection, and rational intuition in our appraisal of theories and interpretations—the reason being that those faculties, innate in all normal human beings, give us direct cognitive access to the facts.[3] Academic learning is to be an exercise of those shared innate faculties.

In Chapter 2 I told the story of some of the upheavals that have taken place in the self-understanding and practice of the academy over the past half-century, the upshot of those upheavals being that the intellectual underpinnings of the traditional view have been undermined. From the work of Thomas Kuhn and Hans-Georg Gadamer there emerged the recognition that, in the nature of the case, neither theory-choice in the natural and social sciences nor interpretation in history and the humanities can be made by reference solely to the value of fidelity to the facts to which perception, introspection, and rational intuition give us cognitive access. Additional considerations do and must play a role—in natural science, simplicity, elegance, explanatory power, conservatism, and the like; in history and the humanities, significance.[4]

What also served to undermine the traditional view

was growing recognition of the fact that, while the values that shape theory-choice in the natural sciences may, for the most part, be shared in common by those who work in those disciplines, that is by no means the case for the social sciences and the humanities. The point is especially evident for history. Every historical narration is necessarily suffused with judgments of significance, and it is clear to everyone that, in our pluralist society, those judgments of significance do not enjoy consensus. One man's significance is another man's irrelevance.

A fundamental assumption of the Enlightenment was that, in conditions of freedom, fundamental convictions concerning God, the good, and the right would tend to converge; what keeps us apart is devious and oppressive priests and preachers. By contrast, one of the assumptions behind the work of the Harvard political philosopher John Rawls was that, in conditions of freedom, fundamental convictions concerning God, the good, and the right tend to *diverge;* society as a whole becomes pluralized with respect to such convictions.[5] This seems to me indubitably correct. The academic sector of society is not insulated against this development. In a liberal democratic society, academic learning, especially in the social sciences and the humanities, tends in the direction of pluralization—unless hegemonic pressures are exerted in favor of certain positions over others.

Let me attach a gloss at this point, lest conclusions be drawn that I would firmly resist. From the developments I have traced, and with which I have aligned myself, some draw the conclusion that there is no structured reality, independent of human minds, for us to find out about, explain, and interpret. From this they conclude, in turn, that truth, understood as correspondence between truth-bearers and truth-makers, cannot be a goal of the academic enterprise. The moral some draw is that the goal of the academic enterprise is to solve problems,[6] or to come up with theories and interpretations that prove interesting. Others draw the more radical conclusion, that we must shed our illusions and recognize that the academy is, at bottom, a constellation of forces. Power is the name of the game.

No such conclusions follow from anything I have affirmed. The lessons to be drawn from the story I have told pertain not to ontology but to our understanding of academic learning and the constitution of the self that engages in such learning. There is a structured reality, independent of human minds. Our goal as practitioners of academic learning is to find out about, explain, and interpret that reality. We seek explanations and interpretations that are, among other things, faithful to the facts, not just those we find personally gratifying or that serve some social cause we embrace.

ACADEMIC LEARNING UNDERSTOOD AS INTERPRETATION

Let me now cast these points in a somewhat different light. Academic learning, whatever else it may be—discovery, explanation, hermeneutic understanding—is an *interpretive* enterprise. By this I mean that it is never just a matter of opening oneself to reality; always it requires a positive contribution on our part. To use Kant's language: it's a blend of receptivity and spontaneity—an engagement between a structured reality and a structured self, each making an indispensable contribution to the engagement. The contribution of the self to the engagement is what I call *interpretation.*

One point at which interpretation takes place, to which I have not yet called attention, occurs in the exercise of perception and introspection themselves; even here, we do not escape interpretation. For perception and introspection typically take place *under concepts;* and concepts are, of course, a contribution of the self. I perceive the creature before me *as,* say, a flying squirrel. The idealists were right in their insistence, against the empiricists, that conceptual interpretation does not just come *after* perception and introspection, in the form of beliefs they evoke in us, but occurs *within* perception and introspection.[7]

I must add, again to forestall misunderstanding, that the fact that one's exercise of perception and introspection is under concepts does not imply that one is not thereby gaining cognitive access to the facts; even less does it imply that those facts are not independent of human minds. Suppose that I perceive what I am seeing *as* a flying squirrel, in other words, that I perceive it *under the concept of* flying squirrel. Suppose, further, that it is in fact a flying squirrel. If so, then, in perceiving it under the concept of flying squirrel I perceive it as what it is, namely, a flying squirrel. Sometimes concepts block cognitive access; mostly, they enable it. Lacking the concept of a flying squirrel, I could not see the thing before me *as* a flying squirrel, which is what it is, nor could I form the belief that it is a flying squirrel. The fact that academic learning is an interpretive enterprise is not incompatible with its being aimed at discovering what is true in the light of what is judged to be important.

ACADEMIC LEARNING AS A SOCIAL PRACTICE

In the second chapter of this book I noted that, before the developments I traced there got under way, *Wissenschaft* (academic learning) was often discussed as if it were a Platonic form that slowly gets instantiated in the course of history, far and away the best of its instantiations being, so it was thought, mathematics and modern natural science. Philosophers talked about what they called "the logic" of science. To rethink academic learning along the lines I have traced requires giving up this Platonic way of thinking.

How should we think instead? I suggest that we think of academic learning as a *social practice*, conceiving of a social practice along the lines sketched by Alasdair MacIntyre in his well-known discussion of social practices in *After Virtue*. Characteristic of a social practice is that those who engage in the practice do so in the expectation of thereby achieving certain goods, among them, goods not otherwise achievable, and that they do so with certain criteria in mind for competent engagement in the practice, criteria that they employ in guiding their own engagement and in evaluating that of themselves and others, these criteria for competence being more or less closely connected to the goods aimed at. What is furthermore characteristic of a social practice is that it is both susceptible to changes across time in goals and criteria for competence, and susceptible at a given time to different practitioners employing somewhat different goals and criteria for competence—and to controversies among those disagreeing practitioners. What accounts for the changes and differences in goals and criteria is highly diverse: new technological developments, problems and conundrums that arise within the discipline, new discoveries, new developments in religion, new developments in philosophy, great feats of intellectual imagination on the part of individuals, new social concerns—on and on. Last, characteristic of a social practice is that it is a tradition, in the sense that learning how to engage in the practice takes the form of one's forebears in the practice handing on to one how it is to be done. From one's teachers—sometimes themselves prac-titioners, sometimes not—one learns the goals, the cri-teria for competence, and the skills presupposed by ap-plication of those criteria; along the way one also learns how to participate in the controversies over goals and criteria.

The developments of the past half-century, in the self-understanding of the academy that I traced, make it compelling to think of academic learning like that: as a norm-laden and purposeful social practice, variable and conflictual with respect to norms and purposes. The pe-rennial presence of disagreements over the goods to be achieved and over the criteria of competence to be em-ployed, and the periodic eruption of deep and sustained controversies over such matters, are not marks of a break-down in the practice but indicative of the extraordinary openness of the practice of academic learning to new and divergent interests, values, and convictions.

The Role-Ethic of the Scholar

In my opening chapter I described the traditional under-standing of the role-ethic of the practitioner of academic learning. The most fundamental component in the traditional understanding was that practitioners are to discipline themselves to employ, in their evaluation of theories, only the deliverances of perception, introspection, and rational intuition, plus that bit of testimony whose reliability has been confirmed on the evidence of those deliverances. They are to become objective in that way, eliminating all particularist bias as they direct their inquiries in accord with the internal dynamics of the discipline and use only the value of fidelity to experienced and rationally intuited facts in their acceptance and rejection of theories and interpretations. Those who conform to that ethic can reasonably expect that disagreement on some matter will eventually be dispelled. Disagreement is a sign that someone is not properly employing their faculties of perception, introspection, or rational intuition— or a sign that they have allowed values other than the value of getting at the facts and their interrelationships to intrude.

Dialogic pluralism is what I call the role-ethic of the practitioner on the alternative understanding of academic learning that I am suggesting.[8] Let me describe it. One enters the academy as who one is—formed as one has been formed, making no attempt to become what one cannot become, viz., The Human Being Itself. One enters as someone who possesses human nature, of course, but also as someone who exhibits the particularities of a contingent character-identity and orientation: male or female, gay or straight, Caucasian or African American, rich or poor, Christian or Buddhist. To enter the academy is to participate in an ongoing social practice together with persons of diverse character-identities who embrace different comprehensive orientations. The old reason for excluding religious orientations, namely, that they are intrinsically nonrational, is no longer tenable—it never was!

Amidst all the variations in identities and orientations, many if not most of the participants share one deep goal, however: to discover the facts in certain domains of reality and to arrive at theories and interpretations that both are faithful to those facts and satisfy one's values and judgments of significance. Truth suffused with significance is their shared goal.

Something else is shared by these participants, amidst all the variations in identities and orientations, namely, when differences arise on significant matters, the offering to each other of reasons, reasons against the position of the other person, reasons for one's own position. The academy is pervaded by the offering of reasons. The reasons might point to beliefs one shares with one's interlocutor, or to experience or testimony of some sort, or to "intuitions."

The goal of this interchange of reasons is to arrive at agreement on the matter at hand. One starts from dissensus and aims at consensus—living with the reality that often one does not achieve the agreement one aims at and hopes for because the segment of reality under consideration is complex and baffling, or because prejudices are getting in the way, or because different character-identities lead the parties to see things in distinctly different ways, and so forth. Even when agreement is not achieved, however, there may be value in the exchange of reasons. The parties may understand each other better than they did previously, understand why the other party holds the position she does hold. Such mutual understanding is of worth.

Implied in what I have been saying is that the participants don't just *offer* reasons to each other but also *listen* to reasons, listen to them with an open mind. One may believe, about some quarter in the academy, that nothing worth listening to is coming from there. But one arrives at that judgment after having listened, and one keeps one's ear cocked on the off chance that one might be surprised. When a religious person enters the dialogue, she doesn't just talk, she listens, thereby exposing herself to critique, and to the real possibility that she may be led to change some of her beliefs. She does not immunize her beliefs against critique.

As both speakers and listeners, we engage our fellows in recognition of their cognitive capacities and ours, and of their fallibility and ignorance and ours. *Dialogic pluralism.* The New Critic literary scholar engages in dialogue with the Marxist critic. Feminist theorists engage in dialogue with those who hold that gender should be irrelevant to scholarship. Those who view religion as a mere epiphenomenon engage in dialogue with those who are convinced that religion is a fundamental explanatory factor in human affairs. And so forth.

There is more to engaging in academic learning than participating in a dialogue: one learns languages, reads poetry, performs experiments, makes observations, works out one's own views. But the overarching character of the enterprise is an ongoing multifaceted dialogue or conversation; and the relevant role-ethic is the ethic of one who engages in a conversation—a civil conversation, let me add. It's a dialogue in which one starts from difference and disagreement and pursues agreement by offering and listening to reasons.

Among the matters that are the topic of arguments are criteria for competence; the standards of the guild are not established in the Platonic heaven. Important as it is to recognize this point, it is equally important not to exaggerate its importance. It often happens that persons and groups in the academy who argue vigorously with each other, but find themselves still disagreeing at the end of the day, nonetheless agree that each party has conducted the argument competently.

The ideal that inspired the old understanding of the role-ethic of the scholar was objectivity. The ideal that inspires this alternative understanding is honor and fairness. I myself have no idea what it would be like for a philosopher to be objective; nothing comes to my mind when I try to imagine what that might look like. But I do know what it's like to pay to the other participants in a philosophical dialogue the honor of taking their views seriously and treating them fairly.

Religions as Comprehensive Interpretations

In the preceding chapter I noted that the understanding of religion typically held by those who charge religious people with suffering from a "rationality deficit" is that religion, at its core, consists of beliefs about the transcendent—God and the afterlife—and that those beliefs are typically not held on the basis of arguments. Or if they are held on the basis of arguments, the premises of the arguments are internal to the person's religious belief system. The critic claims that holding them in that way represents a malfunction or misuse of one's capacity for reasoning, hence, the charge that religious people suffer from a rationality deficit.

Rather often, those who think of the beliefs of religious people as primarily beliefs about the transcendent regard those beliefs as add-ons to beliefs about the nontranscendent. All of us, religious and nonreligious alike, have beliefs about the nontranscendent—some true, some false, some entitled, some not entitled. Religious people, so it is thought, add on beliefs about the transcendent whereas secular people make do without that add-on.

In the preceding chapter, I hinted at my disagreement with this add-on picture but I did not directly challenge it; I focused on responding to the charge that not holding one's religious beliefs on the basis of arguments constitutes a malfunction or misuse of one's capacity for reasoning. It's time to challenge the understanding of religion as primarily add-on beliefs about the transcendent.

I judge that Wittgenstein's most important contribution to our understanding of religion, in his provocative, but brief and scattered, remarks on the topic, was his calling to our attention how distorted is the view of religion as add-on beliefs about the transcendent. He says in one place, "It strikes me that a religious belief could only be something like a passionate commitment to a system of reference. Hence, although it's *belief*, it's really a way of living, or a way of assessing life. It's passionately seizing hold of *this* interpretation. Instruction in a religious faith, therefore, would have to take the form of a portrayal, a description, of that frame of reference, while at the same time being an appeal to conscience."[9] Religions vary greatly in how comprehensive they are. But typically they are, indeed, what Wittgenstein calls "a way of living": a way of apprehending reality, of thinking, of feeling, of "assessing life," a way of engaging one's fellow human beings and the natural world. In my opening chapter I used the term "orientations." Religions are orientations—*comprehensive* orientations.

Recall, from the preceding chapter, William Alston's analysis of one of the mystical experiences that William James reported in his *Varieties of Religious Experience.* The person who had the experience described it as the experience of apprehending or perceiving God. He did not describe himself as adding on to his experience a belief about God; he described himself as apprehending God. In short, he *interpreted* his experience in a certain way—a *theistic* way, if you will.

I suggest that intrinsic to every religion is a characteristic way of interpreting certain segments of experience and reality—that is, nontranscendent, immanent, mundane reality. Not theistic add-ons to what is believed about experience and immanent reality, but *interpretations* of experience and immanent reality. Religions are more than that, of course. Most of them do incorporate beliefs about the transcendent, and all of them incorporate certain practices. But all of them incorporate interpretations of experience and immanent reality. The religion of ancient Israel incorporated the interpretation of Israel's escape from slavery in Egypt as God's deliverance. Christianity incorporates the interpretation of the execution of Jesus of Nazareth and his subsequent appearances as God's vindication of Jesus' authority. The religion of the person who offers grace before meals incorporates the interpretation of the food before him as a gift from God. On and on it goes: intrinsic to religions are interpretations of experience and immanent reality— ways of apprehending and thinking about those.

Recall the lines from John Berryman with which I began the first chapter:

> Master of beauty, craftsman of the snowflake,
> inimitable contriver,
> endower of Earth so gorgeous & different from the
>   boring Moon,
> thank you for such as it is my gift.

What comes to speech here is Berryman's interpretation of the beauty of snowflake and earth, and of his own poetic gift, as the handiwork of a cosmic craftsman, worthy of praise and thanks on that account.

In his much-discussed book *A Secular Age*, Charles

Taylor engages in extended critique of the understanding of religion as an add-on, arguing at length that one cannot just peel off a person's religious beliefs from the totality of his beliefs and be left with beliefs that he shares with his secularist fellows. Taylor argues that secularism is itself a distinct, anti-religious interpretation of experience and reality. The religious person interprets things differently from how a secularist interprets those same things. I refer those who want an extended critique of the add-on understanding of religion to Taylor's book.

RELIGION AND SCHOLARSHIP
ARE BOTH INTERPRETATIONS

The reader can now see where we are headed. When reflecting on the nature of academic learning, we saw that scholarship is an interpretive social practice, and that the convictions and values shaping one's participation in the practice are, to a considerable extent, brought with one from one's life in the everyday rather than emerging from one's participation in the practice of one's academic discipline. What we have just now seen, when reflecting on the nature of religion, is that religions are not just add-on beliefs about the transcendent but incorporate comprehensive interpretations of experience and immanent reality. Secularisms, such as naturalism, humanism, and Marxism, resemble religions in that respect.

If religious interpretations dealt with a distinct dimension of experience and reality, a distinct "religious" dimension, one could then argue that the scholarly articulation of such interpretations should be confined to theological schools and seminaries and kept out of the modern university, on the ground that the modern university should confine itself to "secular" matters. But religious interpretations are not limited in that way. Religious interpretations pertain, in good measure, to the very same dimensions of reality that the academic disciplines deal with: justice, art, moral obligation, persons, our responsibilities to the natural environment, religion itself, on and on.

Or if a religious person's way of thinking about, say, art, was a distinctly different style of thinking from that of other scholars—if it was theology of art—then again one could argue that it has no place in the modern university but should be confined to theological schools and seminaries. But that, too, is not the case. The religious person who is a philosopher of art employs the same philosophical style of thinking as other philosophers of art: same concepts, same ways of arguing, and so on. But though her style of thinking is the same—philosophical, not theological—it's likely that somewhere along the way her religion will lead her to disagree with some of her secular colleagues. If she reflects on the place of art in life—a common topic of discussion among philosophers of art—she will find herself disagreeing with those inspired by the Romantic tradition who hold that art is capable of saving us from what we human beings most deeply need saving from. She will not ascribe salvific powers to art.

An excellent example, in my own field of philosophy, of the sort of religion-shaped scholarship that I have in mind is *Finite and Infinite Goods: A Framework for Ethics*, by Robert Adams, former chair of the Yale philosophy department and now retired.[10] In sustained dialogue with other scholars in the field of ethics and value theory, both historical and contemporary, Adams articulates a theistic framework for ethics and then, in certain areas, goes beyond that to flesh out the framework in rich detail.

Religious Voices in the
Representative University

I have still not directly addressed the main question of this book: what place do nonconformist religious orientations and voices have in the modern so-called secular university? Recall, from our first chapter, what I mean by a *nonconformist* religious orientation. I mean an orientation that leads one, in the course of practicing one's discipline, to disagree with some of the scholarship of some of one's colleagues: their assumptions, their conclusions, their goals and values, their way of treating animals, whatever. A nonconformist voice is what Weber called a "prophetic" voice.

When we brought together our conclusions about the nature of scholarship with our conclusions about the nature of religion, we saw how it is that religion can and does shape the practice of scholarship in the academic disciplines, and why it does not just function as an addendum. It does so in the same way that a feminist orientation can and does shape the practice of scholarship in various disciplines, in the same way that a Marxist orientation can and does shape the practice of scholarship in various disciplines, and so forth. But the university is an institution, not a social practice. So the question remains, whether nonconformist religious orientations and voices are appropriate within that type of educational institution which is the modern so-called secular university, or whether they are only appropriate within theological seminaries and religiously committed colleges and universities. The question does not arise for those whose religious orientation is conformist. It arises for those whose religious orientation is not conformist and who speak, now and then, with a distinctly religious voice.

It's important to keep in mind the social situation of the institutions we are talking about. Recall my comment, at the beginning of my first chapter, that we are not talking about *the university as such*. We are talking about the academic sector within a liberal democracy whose citizens embrace a plurality of comprehensive orientations. More specifically, we are talking about the academic sector within our highly pluralistic *American* liberal democracy.

Far more than is the case for any other liberal democratic society, the academic sector in American liberal democracy comprises the most astonishing diversity of

institutional forms: public universities, private uni\
ties, research universities, community colleges, teacher-
training colleges, liberal arts colleges, professional schools
—and that's just the beginning. Contained within this
diverse mix are those colleges and universities that are
commonly called "secular." Yale is among those. The
fact that among Yale's professional schools is a distinctly
Christian divinity school would be seen, by those who
insist on calling Yale a secular university, as a sign of the
fact that, in Yale's case, the gorgeous butterfly of a fully
secularized institution has not yet fully emerged from
the chrysalis spun by its religious founders three centuries ago.

Setting aside its divinity school for a moment, let's
take a look inside Yale in the early years of the twenty-
first century. The university has a chaplain who, among
other duties, organizes weekly worship services in the college chapel. At commencement, a member of the clergy
offers an invocation, and often a hymn is sung—not
very well, admittedly, because, for some reason, the ones
chosen are usually unfamiliar. There is a course in the
law school on law and the book of Job, another on the
relation between law and theology. There is a seminar in

the philosophy department on the nineteenth-century Protestant theologian Friedrich Schleiermacher, another on the emergence of the classical Western concept of God. There is a course in the English department on Jewish hermeneutics.

I could go on in this vein. But the point is obvious from just this small sample: when one actually looks inside this so-called secular university, one sees that it is not secular—not in any plausible sense of that term. But it is also no longer what it once was, namely, a religiously committed university. It's a *pluralist* university. Not a *neutral* university, in the sense that there is a prohibition on professors speaking in the distinctive voices of their comprehensive orientations or character-identities, but a *pluralist* university, in the sense that voices of a wide variety of orientations and character-identities are heard, religious voices among them, with none enjoying hegemony. Many other American universities are pluralist in the same way Yale is.

Given the manner in which the sector of higher education is constituted in the United States, there is nothing wrong with one institution of higher education committing itself to being Catholic, another committing itself to being Marxist, a third committing itself to being Southern Baptist. In such institutions, one or another orientation or character-identity enjoys hegemony; but in the sector of higher learning as a whole, there remains enormous freedom and diversity. Nobody, to any significant degree, is treated unjustly under such an arrangement. If one does not want to participate in an educational program shaped by, say, Catholicism, one has a wealth of options.

But suppose that an institution in our pluralized society undertakes to be representative—or, to look at it from the other side, undertakes to be nondiscriminatory with respect to the significant comprehensive orientations and character-identities to be found in American society. Then it places itself under obligation to become genuinely pluralist. The voice of the materialist has a place in such an institution, along with the voice of the Marxist and the voice of the humanist; but so too, religious voices have a place. A hegemonic institution is perforce not representative. And the burden of my second chapter was that objective neutrality is not a third option between hegemony and pluralism.

What, for example, would an objectively neutral

telling of the story of the American Civil War look like? The idea makes no sense. Or an objectively neutral philosophical account of the foundations of ethics? Or an objectively neutral telling of the story of the European Enlightenment? The standard telling of the story of the Enlightenment is that it represented release from the bondage of religion, thereby enabling Reason to come into its own.[11] A recent collection of essays, *The Persistence of the Sacred in Modern Thought*, tells a very different story: the major Enlightenment figures, so the authors argue, were deeply religious in their thinking.[12] In a pluralist university, both tellings of the story have their place. From their engagement with each other, a deeper, more subtle, understanding of the Enlightenment may emerge.

A FURTHER EXPLANATION OF PLURALISM

Let me say a bit more about what I mean by a "pluralist" institution, since there are different ways of understanding the idea. An academic institution that allowed the representatives of various comprehensive orientations and character-identities to exist in separate enclaves, each engaged in working out its own views, listening to members of the in-group but ignoring everybody else, confining themselves to discussions with their fellow believers, might, I suppose, be called a "pluralist" institution. There have been such enclaves in recent years—groups claiming, for example, that no one else can understand them because no one else has suffered in the way they have suffered and to the extent they have. A university consisting of such enclaves would be no more than a disparate collection of hegemonic programs, institutes, and departments. It would not be the sort of pluralist university I have in mind; it would not be pervaded throughout by the ethos of dialogic pluralism.

I concede the importance of space in institutions of higher learning for persons and groups to spend time working out their own ideas, paying little attention, for the time being, to objections; only thus is the argument deepened and enriched.[13] But, eventually, the time comes to reenter the pluralist dialogue. That, as I see it, is the role-ethic of the scholar generally. I see it as especially important, for those institutions that undertake to be representative, to promote and uphold this role-ethic. For it is in such a university—where else?—that living proponents of all significant positions are brought together in one grand dialogue, each gleaning from the other what she thinks worth gleaning, each contributing what she thinks worth contributing, with the result that more about ourselves and our world is uncovered, explained, and hermeneutically understood than any party in the dialogue could have achieved by itself.

Some religious persons will refuse to engage in this grand pluralistic multifaceted dialogue: they are convinced that nothing is to be gained by listening or speaking to those outside the faith. Such people have no place in the university that undertakes to be representative; they reject its fundamental ethos. The representative pluralist university is not neutral with respect to the ethic of dialogic pluralism; it is committed to it. Let it be added that religious people do not have a monopoly on arrogant exclusivism!

But doesn't the fact that, in my second chapter, I generalized Gadamer's claim that induction into a certain tradition yields privileged cognitive access to certain segments of reality, imply that we have to tolerate enclave-pluralism? Not at all. The person who has privileged cognitive access to some segment of reality on account of her orientation or character-identity should do what she can to share with others what she has learned, offering reasons, inviting others to share certain experiences. She may fail; she should expect that rather often she will fail. But when she does, she does not glory in the failure but regrets and tries again.

A WORRY

I can imagine a worry that readers might have at this point. Some scholars who are religious prefer not to participate in a pluralist university of the sort I have described. For whatever reason, they don't want to interact with scholars of different orientations from their own. Fair enough. Given the extraordinary diversity of higher education in the United States, it's likely that they can find some religiously committed institution where they will feel at home.

But what about those who do want to work in a pluralist university of the sort I have described? Is a pluralist university that aims to be representative thereby committed to being open to considering, for membership on its faculty, all those religious persons who possess the necessary academic credentials, ignoring whatever fringe views they might hold? Should medical schools consider for membership on their faculties highly qualified candidates who vocally oppose blood transfusions for religious reasons? Should sociology departments consider highly qualified candidates who argue on religious grounds for legalizing polygamy? Readers can easily think of other examples of a similar sort.

Every pluralist university has to deal, on occasion, with cases of this sort: highly competent scholars with fringe views that they are more than happy to debate with colleagues. I don't see that fringe views inspired by religion introduce anything new into the picture. Nationalism inspires fringe views, racism does, Marxism does. Academically qualified persons who hold fringe views are always difficult to deal with. Sometimes the fringe view should be allowed, even encouraged, because it might lead to a new and illuminating way of thinking. Sometimes the fringe view, whether or not inspired by religion, bears, so far as the rest of us can see, no such possibility. Then it's acceptable to exclude it. The pluralist university is not a soapbox open to all comers. Nor, indeed, is any other sort of university.

A FINAL POSITIVE ARGUMENT

The argument I have presented, for the inclusion of religious orientations and voices in the pluralist university
of the modern world that aims to be representative, is
an argument from justice and consistency. My argument
has been that the only option that is fair and consistent
for a university of that sort, in a pluralistic society such
as ours, is that it include religious orientations and voices
within the dialogic pluralism that it promotes. Along
the way, I took note of a common benefit of scholars of
diverse orientations engaging in dialogue with each other,
namely, deeper understanding.

My sense is that this argument from justice and
consistency leaves one feeling not entirely satisfied. Yes,
justice and consistency require it. But what would such
institutions lose if distinctly religious orientations and
voices were excluded from the multifaceted argument
that takes place within them? What would be lost to the
academic sector of American society if distinctly religious orientations and voices were confined to religiously
committed institutions of higher education?

Humanity's religions are too diverse for me to answer this question informatively with all religions in mind. So let me return to where we began, namely, with Weber's inner-worldly ascetic—Christian or Jewish.

The voice of such a person, said Weber, is necessarily absent from the modern university. My discussion has been one long sinuous argument to the effect that he was wrong about that. I sketched the ideal of a genuinely pluralist and representative institution of higher education, committed to the ethos of dialogic pluralism, in which the voice of the academically competent, inner-worldly ascetic is heard along with other academically competent voices—each sometimes speaking in distinctive tones, sometimes in tones that are characteristic but not distinctive. And not only did I sketch the ideal; I noted that this ideal is actualized, to a considerable extent, in the university of which I was a faculty member, Yale University, and in others as well.

What would be lost if the distinctive voice of the Jewish or Christian inner-worldly ascetic were not heard in such a university? The question can be divided: what would the inner-worldly ascetic regard as lost, and what might those who are not inner-worldly ascetics—a diverse group, of course—regard as lost? The latter question is the more relevant here; so that's the one I will address.

I am uncomfortable, however, with trying to speak the mind, on this topic, of those who are not inner-worldly ascetics. As the reader will have surmised, I have been motivated to conduct this long, complex, wide-ranging argument because I am myself one of Weber's inner-worldly ascetics. As such, I much prefer going about my work, speaking in my distinctive voice when that seems appropriate, speaking in a voice that is expressive of my identity as an inner-worldly ascetic but not distinctive when that seems called for—either way, trying to speak in such a way that God will love both the verbs and the adverbs of what I do—and then leave it to those who are of different convictions to say what, if anything, they find of worth in what I said. Who am I to speak for them? Nonetheless, I shall undertake to do so.

Let's have a bit, just a small bit, of what the Jewish or Christian inner-worldly ascetic has to say, both within the academy and outside. She urges us always to be thankfully alert to the excellence that surrounds us: to the beauty of the snowflake, to the wondrousness of the poet's gift, to the joy of loving human relationships. At the same time, she urges us to expand our field of vision to discern, behind all these, a reality of another order whose excellence each thing reflects in its own way and on which each is dependent. She finds herself thinking of this transcendent reality in personal terms; and for her, an implication of the transcendent being personal is that there is nothing of higher worth in dependent reality than persons. Persons are never to be violated.

She sees them violated all about her, abused, oppressed. Something is deeply awry, she concludes; there is a wound in the world. And then she hears what she identifies as a word from the transcendent telling her that this should not be, and calling her, and everybody else, to work for justice. When, in the course of such work, she and her fellows fall into thinking that what is awry is just bad human wills, and that those wills can be corrected by one and another reform program, she once again hears the voice, now telling her, No, it's not all a matter of bad human will; there is a mysterious factor of evil loose in the world. So she resists the temptation to think that by our earnest endeavors we can rid the world of evil. But then, once more, she hears a word from outside our existence, assuring her that tears are not the last word; there is redemption.

As an inner-worldly ascetic myself, I am of the view that something of great worth would be lost to myself and my co-believers if the saying of such things were excluded from the so-called secular university. Not all would be lost; the so-called secular academy is not the only venue for the voice of the inner-worldly ascetic. But the loss would be great.

The question before us, though, is whether there are others than believers who would regard as a loss the disappearance of the voice I have described. Are there others who are repelled by the flatness and shallowness of the professionalized academy and who, on that account, welcome the inner-worldly ascetic's habit of allowing questions of meaning to intrude? Are there others who reject the assumption that we human beings are just DNA and who, on that account, welcome the insistence of the inner-worldly ascetic that we are beings of priceless worth? Are there others who are repelled by humanity's brutality to humanity and to the earth and who, on that account, welcome the inner-worldly ascetic's insistence that justice is a nonnegotiable imperative? Are there others who want the question and the answer of God to be kept alive? I think there are; but as I said, that is for those others to say.[14]

Or is it just a will-o'-the-wisp that I have been pursuing with the complex sinuous argument that I have set out? Is there no real prospect of the university in the modern world being of the sort I am envisaging, an institution in which we not only scurry about solving professional puzzles but also together discuss, from our diverse orientations, the meaning of the mystery, magnificence, and horror of our existence? Is the pluralism of present-day Yale a lingering anomaly?

The shattering events of September 11 produced within the heart and mind of every human being within reach of radio or television a sense of the fragility of our human existence and a longing for justice and redemption. Are that sense and that longing not to be voiced in the university? Are we to preoccupy ourselves with the lenses and lasers of learning? Then we would indeed have become, in Weber's words, nullities, nobodies, "specialists without spirit and sensualists without heart." God forbid that that should be our fate.

NOTES

I

The Traditional Understanding of Religion in the University

1. The eleven addresses are included in Berryman's *Love and Fame,* revised edition (New York: Farrar, Straus and Giroux, 1972), p. 85.
2. I say "so-called secular" because, though a university such as Yale is regularly described as secular, my experience has been that it is in fact pluralist. I will develop this point in Chapter 4.
3. See his *The End of Faith: Religion, Terror, and the Future of Reason* (New York: W. W. Norton, 2005).
4. H. H. Gerth and C. Wright Mills, trans. and eds., *From Max Weber: Essays in Sociology* (Oxford: Oxford University Press, 1970), p. 152.
5. *From Max Weber,* p. 146.
6. *From Max Weber,* p. 146.
7. In my book *Until Justice and Peace Embrace* (Grand Rapids: Eerdmans, 1983), I called the Christian version of Weber's inner-worldly asceticism "world formative Christianity."
8. *From Max Weber,* p. 155.
9. *From Max Weber,* pp. 155–56. Translation slightly altered for the sake of clarity.
10. This has to be qualified to allow for a chain of testimony: on the

evidence of the deliverances of *my* experience and reason *your* testimony is reliable, on the evidence of the deliverances of *your* experience and reason the testimony of S is reliable, etc. The chain has to end with someone reporting the deliverances of his experience or reason.

11. Quoted in Taylor, *Sources of the Self* (Cambridge: Harvard University Press, 1989), p. 224.

12. Quoted in Taylor, *Sources of the Self,* p. 550.

2
Rethinking Scholarship and the University

1. I explain why I disagree in my essay "The World Ready-Made," in my *Practices of Belief: Selected Essays, Vol. 2,* ed. Terence Cuneo (Cambridge: Cambridge University Press, 2010).

2. *The Structure of Scientific Revolutions* (Chicago: University of Chicago Press, 1962).

3. That evidence underdetermines theory was a point already made many years earlier by, among others, the English physicist William Whewell (1794–1866) and the French physicist Pierre Duhem (1861–1916). I do not know why their thought was not part of mainstream philosophy of science in Weber's time. (Stephen Wykstra reminded me of the contributions of Whewell and Duhem.)

4. *The Evolution of Complexity by Means of Natural Selection* (Princeton: Princeton University Press, 1988), p. x.

5. *The Quarks and Captain Ahab; or, The Universe as an Artifact* (Stanford: Stanford University Press, 1997), p. 22.

6. A paraphrase of Pauli by Stuart Kaufman in *Origins of Order: Self-Organization and Selection in Evolution* (New York: Oxford

University Press, 1993), p. vii. This and the preceding two passages were called to my attention by Del Ratzsch.

7. The bibliographical information for this essay is included in note 1 of this chapter.

8. In the wake of Berger and Luckmann's book, a sizable number of things have been said to be socially constructed: danger, quarks, urban schooling, on and on. A witty and wide-ranging discussion of the social-construction fad is Ian Hacking's *The Social Construction of What?* (Cambridge, MA: Harvard University Press, 1999). Especially relevant to our purposes is chapter 3: "What about the Natural Sciences?"

9. The initial English translation of *Truth and Method* was substantially revised for the second edition (New York: Crossroads, 1989).

10. See my *Divine Discourse* (Cambridge: Cambridge University Press, 1995), chapters 8 through 12.

11. I develop a theory of entitlement in my essay "Entitlement to Believe and Practices of Inquiry" in my *Practices of Belief.*

12. I develop this point in my essay "Historicizing the Belief-Forming Self" in my *Practices of Belief,* pp. 118–43.

13. I develop this point about trust in the final chapter of my *Thomas Reid and the Story of Epistemology* (Cambridge: Cambridge University Press, 2001).

3
Rethinking Religion

1. Some critics make the stronger claim, that religion is not just *non*rational but *ir*rational. If the weaker claim fails, as I will argue it does, then the stronger claim also fails.

2. Quoted by Jeffrey Stout, *Democracy and Tradition* (Princeton: Princeton University Press, 2004), p. 176. Not infrequently, sociopolitical aspects of religion are offered as reasons for excluding it from the university. It is said, for example, that religion promotes invidious discrimination and incites violence, and ought to be kept out of the university for those reasons. To arguments of this sort, there is a ready answer: there are many religious people who do not engage in, or promote, invidious discrimination or violence. So why exclude them? And religion is by no means unique in promoting invidious discrimination and inciting violence; secularisms of various sorts do so as well—Marxism and nationalism, for example. So why single out religion for exclusion?

3. There are, no doubt, borderline cases in which it's not clear whether one's capacity for reasoning is not functioning properly or whether it is not being used properly.

4. See, for example, George Marsden, *The Outrageous Idea of Christian Scholarship* (Oxford: Oxford University Press, 1997).

5. "Proposition" is the term favored by philosophers for the object of those beliefs that are of the type *believing that so-and-so*, for example, believing that it is soon going to rain. The words "that it is soon going to rain" name the proposition believed. Other types of belief, with objects other than propositions, are believing a person, believing in a cause, and believing, about something, that it is such-and-such.

6. Why a person's religious beliefs are assumed to be nonrational if the arguments on the basis of which she holds her beliefs only employ, as premises, other religious beliefs, is a nice question. William P. Alston, in *The Reliability of Sense Perception* (Ithaca: Cornell University Press, 1993), argues that it is true, in general, of

large-scale belief-forming dispositions and practices that their reliability cannot be defended with arguments whose premises come from outside the practice. He argues the point in detail for our formation of perceptual beliefs. The arguments that philosophers have offered for the reliability of sense perception all prove, on close inspection, to be circular.

7. See Alvin Plantinga and Richard Taylor, *The Ontological Argument, from St. Anselm to Contemporary Philosophers* (Garden City, NY: Anchor Books, 1965), and the tenth chapter of Alvin Plantinga, *The Nature of Necessity* (Oxford: Clarendon Press, 1979).

8. See his *The Existence of God* (Oxford: Oxford University Press, 1979). A comprehensive up-to-date introduction to recent formulations of the cosmological arguments is Yujin Nagasawa, *The Existence of God: A Philosophical Introduction* (New York: Routledge, 2011). Two excellent collections of essays on natural theology are William Lane Craig and J. P. Moreland, eds., *The Blackwell Companion to Natural Theology* (Oxford: Blackwell-Wiley, 2012), and Russell R. Manning and John H. Brooke, eds., *The Oxford Handbook of Natural Theology* (Oxford: Oxford University Press, 2015). For those who can read Dutch, a fine presentation of where the discussion stands at present is Jeroen de Ridder and Emanuel Rutten, *En dus bestaat God: De beste argumenten* (Amsterdam: Buijten & Schipperheijn, 2015).

9. Plantinga is a Fellow of the American Academy of Arts and Sciences, a former president of the American Philosophical Association (Central Division), and Emeritus Professor of Philosophy at the University of Notre Dame. Swinburne is Emeritus Professor of Philosophy at Oxford University.

10. There are exceptions, for example, Sean Carroll, *The Big Picture:*

On the Origins of Life, Meaning, and the University Itself (New York: Dutton, 2016). Carroll's book is a fine example of a comprehensive physicalist worldview.

11. This would be true for some of the so-called cosmological and teleological arguments, but not for the ontological argument.

12. To most people, quantum electrodynamics—to take just one example—is even more inaccessible than the content of some purported private revelation. Not only can laypeople not access quantum electrodynamics in the way specialists in the field can; they cannot even understand it. In most cases, those who are not the recipient of some purported revelation can, nonetheless, understand its content when it is reported to them.

13. In Chapter 1, when discussing the indispensable role of tradition in science, I noted that most scientists also hold most of their scientific beliefs on the basis of testimony.

14. Whereas most of the propositions that we hold to be true of the natural world emerged from the work of scientists, most of the things established by the theistic arguments were either already believed by religious persons or are sophisticated formulations of what they already believed. So far as I can see, this difference does not have a bearing on the questions I am posing in the text above.

15. In his fascinating little book *On Some of the Characteristics of Belief: Scientific and Religious: Being the Hulsean Lectures for 1869* (1870; reprint, Bristol: Thoemmes, 1990), the nineteenth-century English philosopher John Venn wrote: "We are all of us in a position in which we can know but little even of the facts in most sciences, and next to nothing about the evidences of these facts. This being the case, what is our security against being misled or deceived when we accept a result on the authority of those who

are enquiring at first hand? Except when we possess the evidence afforded by familiar applications or striking predictions, our main reliance must surely be found in the fact that the genuine students are in substantial agreement. If they coincide in their conclusion, we do not doubt that they have arrived at least at some substratum of truth; if they are still in dispute, we mostly withhold our full assent from any one of them" (footnote p. 41; I thank Steve Wykstra for this reference). What Venn says seems to me factually mistaken for students of the social sciences: they firmly believe what some "school" says about social reality even though they are well aware that it is contested.

16. The only philosopher in the modern tradition who discussed the epistemology of testimony was the eighteenth-century Scots philosopher Thomas Reid. I discuss Reid's contribution in chapter 7 of my *Thomas Reid and the Story of Epistemology* (Cambridge: Cambridge University Press, 2001).

17. *Testimony: A Philosophical Study* (Oxford: Oxford University Press, 1995). More recent discussions of the epistemology of testimony are Sanford Goldberg, *Relying on Others* (Oxford: Oxford University Press, 2010), Benjamin McMyler, *Testimony, Trust, and Authority* (Oxford: Oxford University Press, 2011), and Jennifer Lackey and Ernest Sosa, *The Epistemology of Testimony* (Oxford: Oxford University Press, 2006).

18. A beginning is Stephen Wykstra's essay "Toward a Sensible Evidentialism," in William Rowe and William Wainwright, eds., *Readings in the Philosophy of Religion,* 2nd edition (New York: Harcourt Brace Jovanovich, 1989), pp. 426–37, and Wykstra's essay "Not Done in a Corner: How to Be a Sensible Evidentialist about Jesus," *Philosophical Books,* 43 (April 2002), 92–116.

19. The philosophers who first pressed these questions were William P. Alston, Alvin Plantinga, and myself in our essays in the collection *Faith and Rationality: Reason and Belief in God*, ed. Alvin Plantinga and Nicholas Wolterstorff (Notre Dame: University of Notre Dame Press, 1983).

20. The term was introduced by Alvin Plantinga in his essay "Reason and Belief in God," included in *Faith and Rationality*.

21. Beliefs held on the basis of testimony are also held immediately.

22. The thesis that religious beliefs do not, in general, have to be held on the basis of arguments to be rational was called "Reformed epistemology" by Plantinga, on the ground that some theologians in the Reformed Protestant tradition of Christianity had intuitively affirmed the thesis. The name has stuck. In my essay "Reformed Epistemology" I presented the arguments for Reformed epistemology that had been developed up to that point, corrected some misunderstandings, and replied to some objections. The essay is included in D. Z. Phillips and Timothy Tessin, eds., *Philosophy of Religion in the Twenty-First Century* (New York: Palgrave, 2001).

23. For more on the relation between Locke's position and that of the medieval philosopher-theologians, see my essay "The Migration of the Theistic Arguments from Natural Theology to Evidentialist Apologetics" in my *Practices of Belief*, pp. 173–216.

24. I have discussed his epistemology in detail in *John Locke and the Ethics of Belief* (Cambridge: Cambridge University Press, 1996).

25. The thesis, concerning beliefs of a certain sort, that they possess a certain epistemic merit—justification, warrant, whatever—only if they are themselves certain for one or properly based on beliefs

that are certain, has come to be called *classical foundationalism* concerning such beliefs. Locke was a classical foundationalist concerning moral and religious beliefs.

26. The best rehearsal of these failed attempts is William P. Alston, *The Reliability of Sense Perception*.

27. If our topic in this chapter were Locke's epistemology of religious belief, we would want to explore whether he could still maintain his thesis, that we need to hold our religious beliefs on the basis of arguments, if he relaxed his criterion of certitude in such a way as to count certain perceptual beliefs as certain, or if he relaxed his strenuous account of what it is to do one's best.

28. *Critique of Practical Reason*, Akademia volume 5, pp. 162–63. The sentence was inscribed on Kant's tombstone.

29. Quoted from Earl Conee and Richard Feldman by Trent Dougherty in his Introduction to his edited volume *Evidentialism and Its Discontents* (Oxford: Oxford University Press, 2011).

30. Quoted in Dougherty, *Evidentialism and Its Discontents,* p. 7. The essays collected in Dougherty are an excellent sample of the controversies.

31. *Perceiving God* (Ithaca: Cornell University Press, 1991).

32. I defend this principle in my essay "Can Belief in God Be Rational if It Has No Foundations?" in Plantinga and Wolterstorff, eds., *Faith and Rationality.*

33. A point that has not been developed in the recent literature, but that certainly deserves to be developed, was made by John Venn in *Some Characteristics of Belief.* Venn observed that whereas evidence for a belief is typically thought of as consisting of a few premises or one or two experiences, when it comes to complex

matters such as religion, it typically consists of a multiplicity of considerations of different sorts, which the believer tries to make sense of. Stephen Wykstra develops the idea with Venn's help in an unpublished lecture, delivered in October 2013 at the Notre Dame Center for Philosophy of Religion, entitled "Resurrecting Faith: Facts, Feelings, and Finding our Religious Way." Wykstra calls such evidence "squishy evidence."

34. Richard Dawkins, in *The God Delusion*, goes farther, claiming that religious beliefs are *scientific theories*: "A universe with a God would look quite different from a universe without one. A physics, a biology where there is a God is bound to look different. So the most basic claims of religion are scientific. Religion is a scientific theory" (London: Bantam Books, 2006), p. 50. For a thorough analysis of Dawkins's claim that religion is a scientific theory, see Kelly James Clark, *Religion and the Sciences of Origins* (New York: PalgraveMacmillan, 2014), chap. 1.

35. On whether theism is a theory, see the special issue of *Topoi: An International Review of Philosophy* on the topic (vol. 14, no. 2, September 1995). The issue includes an introduction by Paul Draper and contributions by William J. Wainwright, D. Z. Phillips, Stephen J. Wykstra, Stephen Maitzen, William P. Alston, and James F. Sennett.

36. *Lectures and Conversations on Aesthetics, Psychology, and Religious Belief,* ed. Cyril Barrett (Berkeley: University of California Press, 1966). I discuss Wittgenstein's views on religion in some detail in my essay "Are Religious Believers Committed to the Existence of God?" in my *Practices of Belief,* pp. 350–71.

37. Quoted in my "Are Religious Believers Committed to the Existence of God?" p. 358.

38. Wittgenstein, *Lectures and Conversations on Aesthetics, Psychology, and Religious Belief* §30e.

39. Quoted in Alston, *Perceiving God*, pp. 12–13.

40. For a good discussion of the importance of "seemings" in epistemology see Chris Tucker, ed., *Seemings and Justification* (Oxford: Oxford University Press, 2013).

41. It is not true for Plantinga's formulation of the ontological argument.

42. If certain natural laws were varied ever so slightly, life would be impossible. One of the best treatments of the fine-tuning argument is by Robin Collins, "The Teleological Argument: An Exploration of the Fine-Tuning of the Universe," in Craig and Moreland, eds., *Blackwell Companion to Natural Theology*.

43. The developments I have traced could also be narrated from different angles than the one I have adopted here, namely, as responses to the charge that religious beliefs are not rational. I have myself narrated the developments from somewhat different angles in my essays "Epistemology of Religion" in John Greco and Ernest Sosa, eds., *The Blackwell Guide to Epistemology* (Oxford: Blackwell, 1999), and "Religious Epistemology" in William J. Wainwright, ed., *The Oxford Handbook of Philosophy of Religion* (Oxford: Oxford University Press, 2005).

   A result of tracing the developments from the angle of what we can learn from them about the rationality of religious belief has been that I have not mentioned one of the most important books in the area of the epistemology of religious belief, namely, Alvin Plantinga's *Warranted Christian Belief* (Oxford: Oxford University Press, 2000).

44. Richard Rorty, *Philosophy and Social Hope* (London: Penguin Books, 1999), p. 172.

4
Religion in the University

1. Czeslaw Milosz, *The Land of Ulro*, trans. L. Iribarne (New York: Farrar, Straus, Giroux; 1984), pp. 98–99. The translation of Mickiewicz's poem is by W. H. Auden.

2. Recall our argument in Chapter 2.

3. A qualification was always taken for granted, namely, that the content of testimony that has been confirmed for its reliability on the evidence of the deliverances of perception, introspection, and rational intuition can also be utilized.

4. A scientist-turned-philosopher who made essentially the same point as Kuhn and Gadamer was Michael Polanyi in *Personal Knowledge: The Tacit Dimension* (Chicago: University of Chicago Press, 1958). For reasons I do not understand, Polanyi's work never acquired the same influence as that of Kuhn and Gadamer.

5. See his *Political Liberalism* (New York: Columbia University Press, 1993).

6. That is the view Thomas Kuhn espoused in the concluding pages of his *The Structure of Scientific Revolutions*.

7. I can perceive the creature before me under a certain concept—as a flying squirrel—without having a name attached to the concept. That's what happens when someone discovers a hitherto unknown species and then, later, gives it a name.

8. My friend Richard J. Bernstein calls it *engaged fallibilism*.

9. Ludwig Wittgenstein, *Culture and Value* (Chicago: University of Chicago Press, 1980), §64e.

10. *Finite and Infinite Goods: A Framework for Ethics* (Oxford: Oxford University Press, 1999).

11. An elaborate recent telling of this story is two books by Jonathan Israel: *Enlightenment Contested: Philosophy, Modernity, and the Emancipation of Man 1670–1752* (Oxford: Oxford University Press, 2011), and *Radical Enlightenment: Philosophy and the Making of Modernity 1650–1750* (Oxford: Oxford University Press, 2001).

12. Chris L. Firestone and Nathan A. Jacobs, eds., *The Persistence of the Sacred in Modern Thought* (Notre Dame: University of Notre Dame Press, 2012).

13. The point is developed by Imre Lakatos in several of his writings. See, for example, his essay "Falsification and Scientific Research Programs" in Imre Lakatos and Alan Musgrave, eds., *Criticism and the Growth of Knowledge* (Cambridge: Cambridge University Press, 1970).

14. I think here of the fascinating speech by C. Wright Mills that he calls "A Pagan Sermon," in which he says what he, a secular intellectual, hopes to hear from ministers. The application to what he hopes to hear from his fellow academics who are Christian and Jewish "inner-worldly ascetics" is easy to make. The speech can be found in his book *The Causes of World War Three* (New York: Simon & Schuster, 1958). This "pagan sermon" was called to my attention by Chris Eberle.

INDEX

Academic learning, as interpretation, 122–24; as social
practice, 124–26

Adams, Robert, his *Finite
and Infinite Goods* as
excellent example of
religion-shaped scholar-
ship, 138

Alston, William P., *Perceiving
God,* 101; his understanding of religions as interpretations of experience,
109–110, 134

Aquinas, Thomas, theology
to be based on arguments,
88

Argument, explanation of
use of the term, 72

Augustine, St., on believing
in order to know, 58–59

Baxter, Richard, on throwing
off care for external
goods, 16, 28

Berryman, John, first of
"Eleven Addresses to the
Lord," 3, 135

Coady, A.J., work on
epistemology of testi-
mony, 82

Dialogic pluralism, ex-
plained, 127–31

Evidence, experiential, 95;
propositional, 72; testi-
monial, 96

Evidentialism concerning religious beliefs, use of the term, 86; questioning the use of the term, 94–97

Experiential evidence for religious beliefs, 95–102

Gadamer, Hans-Georg, theory of interpretation, 40–45, 119

Hall, Joseph, "God loveth adverbs," 25–26

Hume, David, account of inductive inference, 57–58

Immediate belief, examples of, 84–85; explanation of concept of, 72

Kuhn, Thomas, theory of scientific revolutions, 36–37, 119

Locke, John, argument for holding that religious beliefs must be based on arguments, 86–87; why his argument is unsuccessful, 93–94

MacIntyre, Alasdair, on social practices, 124–5

Mickiewicz, Adam, his ballad "The Romantic," 117

Milosz, Czeslaw, on the ballad "The Romantic," 117

Natural theology, recent developments in, 75–76

Non-conformist religious orientation, explained, 30, 139

Non-rationality of religious beliefs, charge of, 63–64, 71–73; challenging the charge of non-rationality, 83–86, 94–102, 104–106;

meeting the charge of non-rationality, 74–82, 103–104

Of True Religion (Augustine), 59

Particularity, acceptance of in the university, 46–52
Perceiving God (Alston), 101
Perkins, William, on fidelity in one's calling, 26
Plantinga, Alvin, formulation of the ontological argument, 76
Pluralist university, explained, 142–47; the positive good of, 149–54; required by justice in a pluralist society, 142–47;
Privileged cognitive access, 43–45; how it works, 53–59
Propositional evidence, explanation of use of the term, 72

Rational intuition, concept explained, 20
Rationality, explanation of the concept of, 63–64
Rawls, John, claim that in conditions of freedom, comprehensive perspectives tend to diversify, 120
Religions, understood as explanatory theories, 107–112; understood as comprehensive interpretations of reality and experience, 132–36
Religious beliefs, explanation of use of the term, 65; charge that they are inaccessible and immunized, 67–69; charge that they are non-rational (see *Non-rationality of religious beliefs*); experiential evidence for, 97–102; immediate religious beliefs, 83–86; objections to understanding religious beliefs as add-ons, 132–33,

Religious beliefs (*continued*)
136; role of testimony in
religious beliefs, 77–82
Representative university,
religion in the, 139–40
Revelation, as basis for
religious beliefs, 67–69
Role-ethic of the scholar,
5–6; 126–31
Rorty, Richard, on the charge
that religion is non-
rational, 113–14

Significance, role of judgments of in history and
interpretation, 41–42,
50–51
*Structure of Scientific
Revolutions* (Kuhn), 36
Swinburne, Richard,
contributions to natural
theology, 76, 110–11

Taylor, Charles, on Puritan
theology, 25; objections

to understanding religious
beliefs as add-ons, 136
*Testimony: A Philosophical
Study* (Coady), 82
Theory underdetermined
by evidence, 35–39
Truth and Method (Ga-
damer), 40

Weber, Max, case against
religion in the university,
7–19, 25–30; concept of
inner-worldly ascetic,
14–19; melancholic anal-
ysis of modernity, 11–19;
understanding of modern
scholarship, 9–10, 19–25,
role of tradition in his
understanding of modern
scholarship, 23–25
Wittgenstein, Ludwig,
opposition to religions
understood as explanatory
theories, 108; religions
understood as interpre-
tations, 133–34

Index